Anatomy Riot

by
Emily Annette Running

Portland, Oregon

Copyright © 2013 Emily Annette Running

All rights reserved. The text of this publication, or any part thereof, may not be reproduced in any manner whatsoever without written permission from the publisher.

Cover image © Alexis Goldstein 2013
Cover design by Hannah Moore and Emily Running
Editing by Lisa Walser and Parker Huey

ISBN:9781494278397

First Edition 2013

Manufactured in the United States of America
10 9 8 7 6 5 4 3 2 1

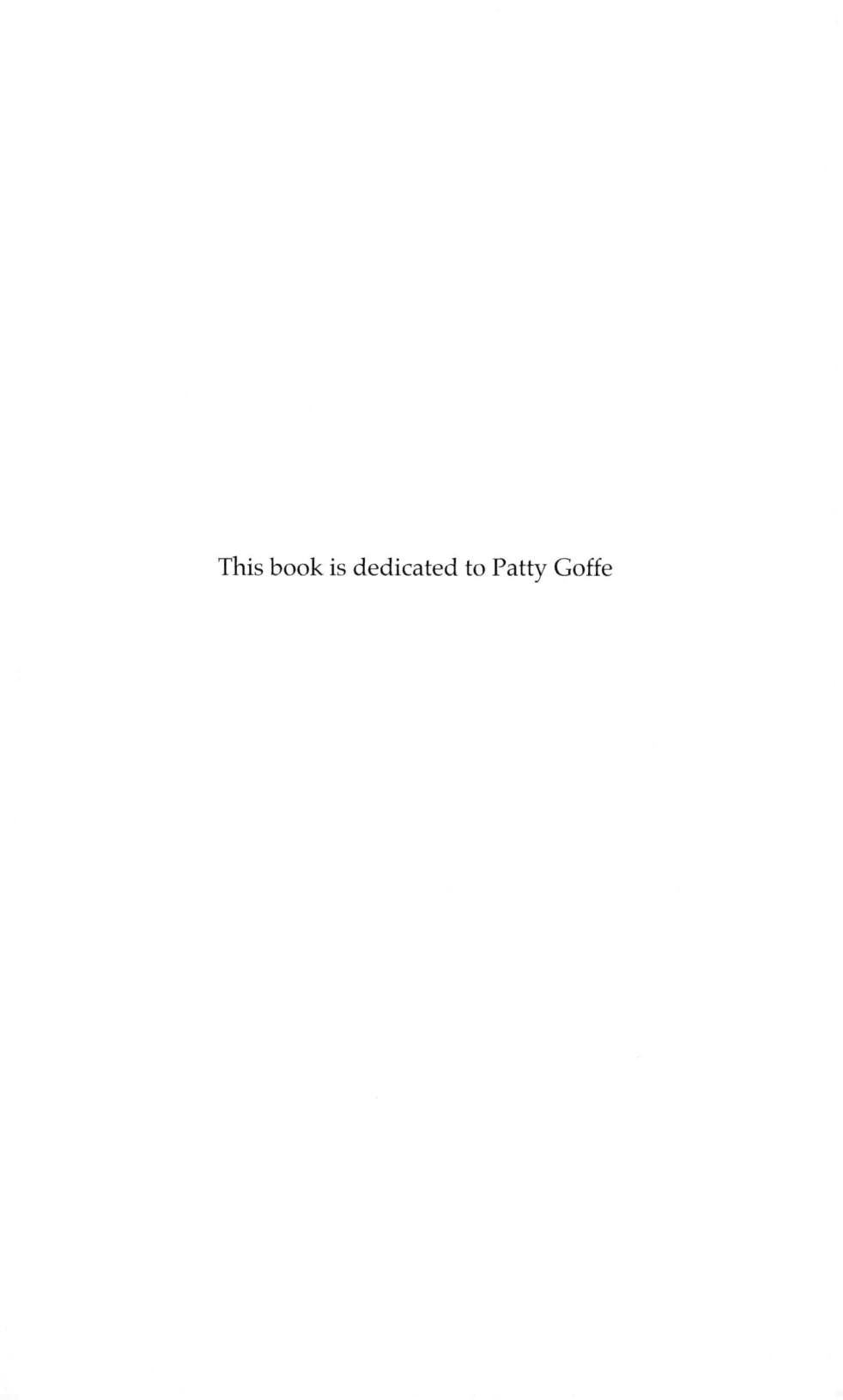

This book is dedicated to Patty Goffe

NOTE FROM THE AUTHOR

I have consulted with many individuals who appear in the book to be sure my facts are straight, though even still there are often multiple sides to the same story, so all I can claim is that this is my rendition. All of the journal entries, notes, and text conversations are indicated as such and have not been changed to preserve their true nature. Friends and family were given the option of taking an alias or embracing the inevitable fame of appearing in my book. He he. All other names were changed.

When I sat down to write this book I had no intentions for it, and I wasn't even sure if it would ever be complete. My only goal was to record my experience from this part of my life before memory washed away the details. Once I began writing I knew it would be an essential part of my process.

I published the ebook version of Anatomy Riot on June 1st, 2013 with no idea if my story was interesting, relevant or if people would be able to connect to it. As readers began relaying their feedback, I was pleasantly surprised to discover that each reader I heard from was able to take something from the book and relate it to their own experience.

If you feel compelled to send me your thoughts I would be delighted to hear them. You may also find yourself interested in seeing photos and videos of some of the things I describe in the book. In either case please visit my website at www.movementinspired.com.

Happy Reading!

TABLE OF CONTENTS

Part One

How did you get into that? 1
Becoming a dancer 3
Becoming an artist 5
Ideal life building 8

Part Two

The first crack in the windshield 12
Contradicting realities 16
Losing trust 19
The scared porcupine 21
Research 23
Kickstand 25
Inkling of clarity 27

Part Three

Thick blackness 30
Raw, exposed 32
Overwhelming gibberish 34
More questions 36
Pure fear 41
The what-ifs 43
Removing the last strip of the mask 44
Preparing for hibernation 46

Wrapping up loose ends 48

Part Four

The second crack in the windshield 52
Redefinition 53
My heart went out to you 55
Identity without affiliations 57
Gut alien 58
Unexpected triumph 59
Paper panic 61
White Bird 64
Public versus private 66
Mile marker 68
Art in the Dark 69
A warm and fuzzy heart 71
It's time 74

Part Five

The big day 76
The other side 80
30 year old granny 83
Bring me a steak 85
Hospital discharge 87
Withdrawal 89
Setting the routine 92
Epic poop 95
First outings 97

Bittersweet transition 99
A day in the life 101
Moment of truth 103

Part Six

The unexpected visitor 106
Always there 109
Digging deeper 114
Trusted advisor 116
Back on the outside 119
No spark 121

Intermission

Part Seven

The flabby tin man 126
Two timing 128
Perpetual nausea 130
Crutches at the gym 132
A halfway new experience in yoga 133
15 weeks 136
The no end in sight black sea 138
My Mumford anthem 140
Dove tail 141
Squeezed and soaked 143
My body was awake 145
Change in strategy 148

Invisible separation 150
Screws 153
No go (go figure) 154
Second time's a charm 155
Left of Center 156
Moving on, moving out 159
No more funding 161

Part Eight

Rhymes with bucket 164
From panic to grounding 166
Soft steps 169
Physical progressions 171
Elusive policy 172
Showtime 175
Still not whole 178
Money 180
Two things 181
What I know 183
New list 185

EPILOGUE

An idea 187
A new main character 189
Impermanence 192

ACKNOWLEDGEMENTS

ADDITIONAL RESOURCES

Part One

How did you get into that?

November 13, 2010

    Twenty-five feet in the air, strategically wrapped up in a long strip of fabric, waiting for my musical cue to fall from the ceiling. I'm wearing a gold unitard, my hair is in a mohawk, the light performs its own dance reflecting off the glitter on my body. The audience can feel something dramatic is about to happen. ... 5, 6, 7, 8... I unravel 20 feet in two seconds, hooking one knee over the fabric to stop my fall. The anticipatory tension of the audience released in an audible gasp, a mixture of both excitement and recognition of danger. An evil grin forms on my face, but only because that's my character. I am playing Zap in "Zip Zap Zoom," an aerial dance show based around fictional superheroes. As I exit the stage a young girl in the audience whispers loudly, "Mommy, is that the villain??"

    When I say I'm an aerial dancer people always want to know, *How did you get into that??*

    I've been a professional dancer for 12 years - modern, ballet, jazz, and contemporary and for the past four years, aerial. My relationship with dance has always been like a romantic love affair navigating through passion, uncertainty, glorification, and disappointment.

    Early on my commitment was fickle at best. Dancing is fun! I'm bored. I feel alive! Pointe shoes make my feet hurt. I might be good at this! I'm obviously not that good at this. What about other activities, do I really have to choose? That was high school.

It should be of no surprise that I didn't know exactly what I wanted in high school. Senior year people always asked, *Well, where are you going to college?* I was playing eenie meenie miney moe with colleges, but when I finally landed on the answer it seemed even less clear! No gut feeling of relief nor disappointment illuminating what I really wanted! I never play for the answer I land on, I play for the reaction to the answer. Now what?

I really wanted them to ask, *So, what do you want to do next?* Aha, the missing piece! Eenie meenie wasn't showing me all the options or rather, I was playing with the wrong question. Had I been given the latter question, my answer would have been more like, *Well I don't know, maybe I should move to New York City and take dance classes and find a company to perform with, or I could dance on a cruise ship, travel the world, be young and independent! I'm 18 the possibilities are endless!* But with no guidance nor greater encouragement towards such wild fantasies, I attempted to fuse the practical with my dreams. So, I went to college and emerged four years later with a BFA in Choreography and Performance in Dance.

***

"If you can be anything else, a doctor, a lawyer, an architect, a physical therapist, anything else at all, and be happy, do it, because otherwise it will never be worth the struggles that come with being a dancer." This comment came from Jacques Heim, a choreographer for Cirque du Soleil and the Artistic Director of Diavolo. Despite his success at that point in his career, he spoke from experience, warning anyone interested in pursuing a career in dance of the physical exhaustion it would entail, the lack of solid income, and even sometimes, a lack of respect for dance as a profession. It wasn't until I met Jacques and worked with Diavolo when I was 25 that the dots all connected and I realized that I didn't choose dance, it chose me. There is something about dance that's essential to the core of my being and I genuinely can't live without it.

Becoming a dancer

"All serious dancers know that complete absorption in the complex physical process of performing — whatever kind of style — can bring with it an ecstatic liberation from thought and self-awareness even while the body is functioning at the highest levels. That complete possession of the dancer by the dance is a rare sight, but it is one that can make watching a performance a near-transcendent experience for the audience too" - Roslyn Sulcas

There are multiple dimensions involved in being a dancer. Physically, similar to other professional athletes, dancers spend long hours practicing movements over and over again, training our muscles to achieve impeccable muscle control and virtuosic flexibility. We cultivate strength and power not simply to the extent of accomplishing a move, but to the point where something like leaping through the air in the splits suddenly looks graceful and effortless, or flying on a trapeze from one knee appears soft and delicate.

Then there is the component of expression, without which, a dancer is simply a movement technician. A truly compelling dancer cultivates a quality of movement such that the onlooker actually feels the emotion just by watching. The thing about using your own body as an expressive tool is there is nowhere to hide, the expression must come from the heart, then there you are...vulnerable, raw, exposed.

In college I did an Independent Study on a practice called Authentic Movement. Authentic Movement consists quite simply of following the body's impulse to move or be still. Twice a week I would go to the studio and explore. At the beginning I felt trapped behind my inhibition, unable to release judgement on the aesthetic of my movement. Initially, my impulse was always to be still, to avoid entering that petrifying territory of moving as my authentic self. The problem was that working from the outside in, so to speak, continued to feel hollow. While the shell of my body moved, there was a vault underneath not willing to reveal its contents. Gradually, over the course of many months spent dancing in a room with only a video camera as an observer, the vault began to open. My impulses were now greeted with curiosity and exploration, versus comparison and judgement. My movement felt richer and more alive. I would get carried away and move from a place of passion, not thought.

<u>Independent Study on Authentic Movement - November 5th, 2002</u>
Today I felt like a small child - although really it was just me at age 21, reveling in my opportunity to move! It felt like this: I was running through a field of white daisies. The field went as far as the eye could see in all directions. I kept getting surprised, though by nothing in particular. I would turn around and a butterfly would land on my nose and it would tickle and make me laugh. I would immediately get distracted and keep moving. I didn't know which direction I was going or what my destination was. Something was leading me and I made no objections. I didn't need to make any effort to follow, I just went. There were moments of deep breaths of fresh air. I was happy, very happy. I wasn't carefree, but rather was on top of everything I cared about, there were no worries. My mind was grounded and at ease although my body was floating. Today this is my world.

Becoming an artist

While in my early 20's I was going through the motions of being a professional dancer yet my career seemed scattered. Deciding that I needed a healthier way to make a living than being a waitress, I got my Pilates certification and began teaching. I enjoy teaching Pilates, it's very linear and precise. In classical Pilates there are definite rights and wrongs involved in doing the exercises. Joseph Pilates, the man who developed the system of exercises called the work "Contrology." As the story is told, Joseph Pilates' father was considered an anatomical specimen, but Joseph himself was a very sickly kid. He solved the problem by sneaking out into the woods and working on the fine tuning of his body. He examined anatomy books and worked to isolate and gain perfect control over each individual muscle. His highly detailed method taught me a lot about the human body and was very applicable to my dancing.

While teaching Pilates was helping to pay the bills, I was still agonizing over the question, "What do you do?" I would get the same claustrophobic please-fit-in-this-small-box feeling that I did when I was asked about college. Why do I have to narrow it down to one title? My initial solution was to create a website that represented the many facets of my profession. I titled the site "Movement Inspired" deciding that was the most accurate categorical representation of what I do.

The last missing piece stifling my ability to truly own up to being a dancer was gaining a comfort level with calling myself an artist. So, at age twenty-six I up and moved to Paris. When I stepped off the plane in a foreign country whose language I didn't speak, with no job, no place to live, and no idea what I was doing, I somehow couldn't have been happier! It was just the type of reckless decision that forces you to feel completely comfortable living without logic.

I explored painting, with my silly watercolor set, as well as by going to see exhibits and galleries of some of the most famous artists of all time. I explored many angles of photography. First, as the one behind the camera simply wanting to capture what I was seeing. Second, I happenstanced into being a model for artistic photographers, because you don't have to work very hard to stumble upon opportunities to be a part of artistic experience in Paris. I also explored writing. My friend, who is a writer, went to a writer's group and would bring the material back to me and we would discuss composition, language use, and emotional reaction.

My experience unfolded quite similarly to how you would paint a watercolor. For example, let's say you are painting a watercolor of a small barn nestled in the woods on a sunny day. Instead of painting the barn, then the forest, adding the horizon and filling in the colors, with watercolor you must start with the lightest color because you can't go back and paint lightness over darkness or your colors become muddied. So, you have to start with the sun itself, then paint the rays of light, then just the portion where they reflect off the trees, the barn, the windows, the doorknob. Highlights first. Then you continue to fill in the colors, shapes and structures, following that same pattern until you have painted your scene.

The French hold their artists and scientists in the highest regard as they are the innovators, inventors, creators, and the ones who shape the identity of the culture. Simply interacting with people of this mindset, as well as my varied artistic experiences, gradually filled in my scene. My resulting picture unveiled a realization that painting, sculpture, writing, poetry, photography and dance all have similar basic guidelines of quality, composition, creative process, and aesthetic. My right brain toolkit was more versatile than I'd thought. Suddenly, the capacity to take my creativity so much further illuminated a whole realm of potential for my career and my future!

While Paris was a grand adventure, I had always intended to move back to the Northwest. I imagined my ideal life to consist of establishing strong roots in one location and then seeking opportunities to gallivant around the globe, pursuing a myriad of mini excursions, but with a place to go home to.

Ideal life building

With my newly found creative perspective and inspiration, I landed in Portland, Oregon, with a plan to establish my ideal life.

Hi Portland, I'm just delighted to be here! I adore how artistic and progressive you are. Small enough that I can make a living, big enough that there's still opportunity. I hear you have a very European vibe which is perfect, I'm secretly European at heart. I bought a scooter too, a hot pink one. I'm saving money so I can be an artist (yep, because that is what I am). I'm also a Pilates teacher, which should fit in well because everyone is so health conscious here. I think this is going to work out, I really do.

I felt alive and in control of the life I was going to shape from scratch. Fueled by my recently acquired understanding of how I could use my creative knowledge, I made very deliberate decisions in the first year.

I was lucky enough to live rent-free with my cousin for the first few months and had very minimal expenses. I found free dance classes to take, and began researching dance companies, making calls to artistic directors, and found myself invited to many company classes or rehearsals. In my search I came across a company called AWOL (Aerial Without Limits) and contacted the artistic director. She spoke with me for an over an hour and then invited me to a dress rehearsal for a show they had coming up called "Art in the Dark." The show is their annual signature show and is held in a park/forest just outside Portland. Since I didn't own a car at that point, I had to borrow someone's car to drive out there. When I arrived, they set up a folding camp chair for me and I watched their dress rehearsal.

One thing that immediately caught my attention was how welcoming everyone was! It was a stark contrast to my experience in LA, where everyone seemed very territorial and competitive. When the dancers weren't on stage they would often come over, introduce themselves, and tell me little tidbits about the show. As they remember it, they were trying to impress me, knowing only that I was a dancer and had just moved here from Paris. As I remember it, I fell in love with the positive nature of their group dynamic, the athleticism of aerial dance, and the phenomenal setting for their show. I auditioned for the company about a month later and at age 27 began my new career in aerial dance!

AWOL became my central focus. The company consisted of 12 women who were all in the same age range as me and became my dear friends. I also saw tremendous growth potential with the company. Eager to begin establishing my career in the dance world, I offered to build the company a new website, and also initiated an Education and Community Outreach Program.

My first year with AWOL we rehearsed in an elementary school gymnasium 30 minutes east of Portland. Toward the end of that year it became clear that we would never reach our growth potential unless we moved to our own space closer to Portland where we could hold classes, provide a home to store our equipment, and a venue to invite people to watch us perform. The timing was critical for us to make this step as budget cuts were forcing the school we were using to discontinue their physical education classes, meaning the gym would no longer be available for our use.

Within a few months we had found a warehouse that met our essential criteria of 30 foot ceilings, and enough square footage to hold an audience. We immediately began offering classes, and before long we had a solid base of students. For a very minimal paycheck and first dibs on any classes I wanted to teach to expand the income potential of the job, I slowly and steadily built up the education program. I was the first paid employee of AWOL, and they even built an office for me in the new space. The first year had many failures as well as triumphs. I was learning as I went.

I was the first teacher for most of the students as I taught most of the intro level classes and continued to work with them as they progressed to more advanced levels.

Aside from my work at AWOL, I did need to fill in my income with other teaching. I already had a 600 hour Pilates certification and went through a 200 hour yoga certification, adding yet another dimension to my movement repertoire. I taught Pilates and yoga classes at the Adidas North American Headquarters.

I had started with one puzzle piece at a time and built and built and built on each one. I was an artist, an athlete, a performer, a teacher, and my own boss. While I still didn't have a singular title to state when asked "What do you do?" I had at least created an identity for myself that felt both cohesive and successful.

Eight years in the making, the career and life I was looking for was all starting to make sense.

And then.

It changed.

Part Two

The first crack in the windshield

Journal Entry - January 23rd, 2011
Since I can't cry on paper, I have to write something and hope it helps. I don't know where to start other than by saying this is the beginning of a huge new chapter in my life and I'm terrified to start it. After dealing with a mysterious on-again off-again "injury" for the past decade, I have finally come to a place where I can't proceed in my profession without doing whatever it takes to get to the bottom of it.

January 13th, 2011

    I'm sitting in the surgeon's office at Oregon Health and Sciences University. It's a beautiful day and from the 14th floor I have an incredible view. As I look down at the park below, I wonder if it's actually more amazing from my vantage point. Just walking through the park you wouldn't notice how elaborately and symmetrically the paths, shrubs, and flowers are laid out. Everything is perfect, structured, and meticulously attended to. I'm trying to breathe in the bright, friendly feel of the park to distract myself, but the sterile picture frame of the office window prevents my mind from being free from why I'm here and what I'm about to hear.

    My primary care physician, Dr. Keating, had sent me to get an MRI weeks before and had already told me the results of the MRI over the phone. The medical terminology sounded like gibberish at that point, so I consulted my friend Amy, who is a physical therapist, to explain what it meant. I have bilateral labral tears, the labrum being the soft tissue that pads the ball and socket joint of the hip. She tells me that the repair consists of arthroscopic surgery (which involves a minor incision and sewing up the tear with a microscope). This procedure is outpatient, so no hospital stay, and it would require about three months healing time to be back in action. The thought of this caused a mild breakdown, imagining the possibility of three months of no dancing, but feeling the relief of finally having a solution to a decade of on-and-off hip pain, I came to terms. Amy is in AWOL with me and had the same surgery a few years ago. She is able to do all the same things as I can do now, so at least I have confidence in my future potential. At the doctor's office I sat there on the crackling tissue paper bed feeling like I had a grasp of what I was going to hear.

The surgeon finally breezes in and with little introduction pulls up my MRI on her screen. She's scanning through it briskly, pointing to various of images that just look like hypercolor blobs. She talks quickly and with a matter-of-fact tone. She knows that I'm a teacher and a dancer, because I made a great effort to plaster my intake form with that information. It is imperative that she understands that she is working with a highly physical person, not someone who sits at a desk all day.

She is skimming over the labral tear stuff as if it is virtually an irrelevant fact. Yes, I have labral tears, and yes, there is a type of surgery to fix it that she performs regularly. But the fact that I have them on both sides raised a red flag. Here, she launches into a whole new deluge of information that I was not expecting to hear. My x-rays show that the tears were caused by hip dysplasia, a malformation of the joint. It's congenital, which means I've had it all my life, and explains why I've been in pain on-and-off for so many years.

She continues, "Considering the dysplasia, the arthroscopic surgery will have about a 30 percent likelihood of success. That's not really something I would even perform as you would just be back in here in two years with the same problem."

I'm confused. So you can't help me? What does this mean? In her flat, casual tone, she segues.

"What will have to happen for the surgery to be effective is we have to fix the dysplasia. I don't perform this kind of surgery, but what you're looking at is a procedure where they break your pelvis, restructure the joint, and screw it all back together. The healing time will be quite a bit longer, a year at minimum. The drawback is this surgery is rare, complex, and quite risky."

Instantly, my body has lost all feeling. My ears are ringing, my vision is hazy, and I'm sweating, a feverish kind of sweat, and I'm shivering because it feels like my blood has completely drained from my body. My brain struggles to make sense of what she's saying, yet I am unwilling to hear it. I involuntarily enter a sparring match with the information. I don't understand. This isn't what she was supposed to be telling me! Rare? Complex? Risky? What about my future!?

I don't know what I'm saying out loud because much of my mental capacity has turned off, but I think the words coming out are similar to that of my internal dialogue which is feisty and resistant. Does she not understand what I do? Does she not know this isn't an option? Does she have zero sense of how extreme an impact this would have on my entire life??

And then, in one brief comment, she confirms all my fears, "Well really, how important is dancing to you?"

And now something inside me really snaps. She is a fool, an idiot. She's a robot, who like a factory worker hacks people up and screws them together, as if they are made of wood or plastic. This can't be a solution for a living body. This is unacceptable!

She has me schedule an appointment with a different surgeon who is supposed to go over the pelvis smashing option with me and who would eventually be the one to perform the surgery if I choose that route. My brain is incapacitated with this information. I obligingly get an appointment with Dr. #2 on the books, too numb to know what else to do.

As I drive home my brain starts racing. I call my mom when I get home and I'm hysterical. Not the crying kind, not the laughing kind, just hysterical. I'm sure my mom is even more confused than me because I'm trying to explain something to her that I don't even understand myself, and there's nothing matter-of-fact about my tone. I go on and on and she has many questions I can't answer. She's always been the calm voice of reason for me, but I sense her helplessness to aid in this circumstance at this particular moment. There's just not enough information.

I call Amy as well, hoping she'll confirm what a hoax the surgeon is and assure me there's a different solution. Despite being knowledgeable in the medical field, she hasn't heard of this procedure (which I can't pronounce anyway) and my insufficient understanding of the information I was given leaves many gaping holes. At the end of my broken summary, Amy takes a deep, audible breath and acknowledges that there is a lot more information to learn before even humoring a decision.

<u>Journal Entry - February 6th, 2011</u>
At this point I don't know enough details to know the exact procedure and timeline that's in my future. All I know is that I feel lost. I feel scared. I continue to process on a daily basis while also trying to maintain enough focus on what I'm doing right now as well. I've found the pain more prevalent in my mind and harder to deal with. It's quite crazy to imagine I've been living with a pretty high degree of pain for so many years! Now that I know the cause of it and the potential procedure involved in fixing it, the pain becomes a constant reminder of what's to come. The pain itself somehow feels more unbearable than before. My emotions are constantly on edge.

Contradicting realities

January 20th, 2011

    I've been asked to teach yoga classes to the Timbers, Portland's Major League Soccer team. They are doing preseason training at the Adidas world headquarters, where I already teach Pilates and yoga. Day One, I am greeted by the strength and conditioning coach who asks how I would like the room set up. I indicate the best way to set up and we unroll a yoga mat for each player and one for me at the front of the class.

    I sit down on my mat and look out at the sea of 25 players and 10 coaches. I suddenly realize that I've been so distracted lately that I forgot to be nervous! I'm about to teach a class of extremely fit (some extremely attractive) pro-athletes. Before I have a chance to let the intimidation get in my head, I begin class. They are adorable! Many are concerned about taking their socks off after having worked out all morning. One of the players circles his mat multiple times, like a puppy, before coming to a seat. Another is standing, looking at me attentively, until I make eye contact. He puts his hands together and says "Namaste," which comes out more as a question than a statement. He is trying to follow appropriate yoga etiquette but seems unsure of what exactly it is.

    I find soccer players to be some of the most dynamic athletes out there. They have speed, strength, agility, and are constantly moving on the field. It is truly a pleasure and an honor to be teaching such a high caliber group. Based on past teaching experience, I've determined that adding a little good-humored competition is a great way to motivate men. Coming up right next to one of the players, I pop down into plank as I instruct.

    "Find your plank. Pull the navel into the spine supporting your weight from underneath. Engage the quads, and really press the hands in to the floor to activate the chest. Everything is active here, distributing the effort throughout the body...." I continue doing the movement exactly as I'm instructing them,"...Now bend the elbows, hugging them towards your ribcage, pause half way down...and press back up...again, going half way down and hold...and press up..." I look to my side and smile innocently. I do this every day and I'm not particularly struggling. The player to my side has a look of pure concentration and his arms are shaking. He might not be as entertained with my light-hearted competition as I am. I sense his relief as I pop up just as easily as I had popped down, and move across the room.

Later, we move into hand stands. As a dancer having extensively studied movement, body mechanics, and the way the limbs connect to the core, I chose to do handstands specifically to challenge the players in how they use their bodies. Putting all your weight in your hands requires strength in the arms and the core, and a trust in your ability to manage your own body weight.

I simultaneously talk and demonstrate. "So, you're going to come on to your hands and feet just like this. Bend your knees and send the hips up in the air. I want your legs to stay bent and close to the core." While in a static moment on my hands I continue, "Use the power of your legs to get your hips centered over your shoulders like this."

I look out at the 25 faces that appear to be silently wondering if I'm a complete lunatic. So I add, "Think of it as an experiment! I don't expect it to be perfect, nor necessarily graceful. The idea is to find the connectivity of the upper and lower body, as well as observe how your body responds to unfamiliar movement. And trust your body! Ok, ready, set, go..."

After a well received Savasana (Corpse Pose), I think class has gone well and I'm relieved. I'm standing at the front of class answering questions when the head coach, John Spencer, comes up to me and says, "I just have to ask, how are you so RIPPED?" I look over my right shoulder, over my left shoulder, to confirm the question was indeed directed to me.

I'm completely stumped at what to say and as I'm trying to come up with any sort of response, he proceeds to ask about my workout regiment...what cardio I do, what I eat. He's actually serious, he thinks I'm in phenomenal shape! It's an enormous compliment coming from the head coach of pro-athletes.

    Driving home after class, I just start sobbing. Underneath there is a rush of devastation. I am strong, fit, able to do many physically impressive things. If you didn't know I was having complications with my body, you never would have guessed it watching me. Am I really willing to give all that up (even if just for a short time if you consider the grand scheme of things)? And considering the risks, is surgery the best choice?

Losing trust

January 26th, 2011

    I'm at AWOL rehearsal and we are preparing for our show coming up this weekend. We've been rehearsing for a couple months, and I feel completely confident with the pieces I will be performing. One of the pieces is a handloop piece. The handloop is literally a loop you put your wrist in and the piece mostly consists of high speed spins and big flights on one arm. When we originally learned the piece, I struggled with a move entitled, the "Meat Hook." Emerging from a one arm spin you reach up with your free arm, do a pull up, pike the legs, and then twist the whole body to the side coming into the "Meat Hook." The centrifugal force from the spin makes it much harder to maneuver the body, and it's taken me a month to be able to accomplish the move consistently, but I finally feel ready to perform it.
    The second piece I'll be performing is in the fabric. Fabric is more complicated because how you wrap in and out of moves is very specific, though I don't consider anything in this particular piece to be very dangerous. I start in an ankle hang with the fabric wrapped around me like a cocoon. The title of the song is "Violence," and has a very strong pulsing beat. On the musical cue, I burst out of the cocoon, climb out of my ankle hang, and wrap my body in for the next move…right hip lock, draw the fabric behind the back, between the legs, over the shoulder…15 feet in the air, I gather the tail of fabric hanging below me and wind up into a very fast spin. My heart is suddenly pounding harder and much faster than the music. My brain is sending alarm signals and my body is resisting the next move where I'm supposed to drop from the spin to one knee. I'm completely wrapped in, I know I've done it correctly, there is zero chance that I could fall to the floor. But fear has consumed me. It's not the fabric I don't trust, it's my body. This move always caused a bit of

pain, but the pain previously had mysterious origins which allowed me to detach from it. Now I know there is genuinely something wrong. Not only that, but it's structural, not just a pulled muscle or tendonitis. I am literally not built right.

I have about 10 seconds to process this rush of fear and realization. I force my body to continue, knowing the muscle memory will get me through. I feel weak, I am behind the music, I get tangled completing the rest of the sequence, and finish the piece sloppily, feeling defeated.

The scared porcupine

I've decided to start going to acupuncture. A good friend of mine goes to someone named Alexis, and she says she is amazing....and may be willing to do a trade. I can't afford to pay out of pocket and my insurance certainly isn't interested in paying. I call Alexis and we set up two times, one for a treatment for me and one for a workout for her.

She is very thorough. Each initial appointment for a patient is two hours so there's time to both talk and treat. Previous to my diagnosis I had been to acupuncture elsewhere, but did not really know the terminology to use to describe what was going on. This time, I could at least state my condition in official language and then dive into the details of the types of things I'm experiencing as a result of it. Though in acupuncture they never just ask, *What do you think is wrong with you?* Instead, they inquire about your digestion, what your stools are like, how your sleep is, things that we wouldn't think to offer up on our own.

Alexis' brochure states, "The acupuncturist's job is one of examination and analysis; it requires discerning a pattern in the chaos of seemingly unrelated symptoms." Oh good, she's expecting chaos. I can easily deliver. It feels good to just tell it how it is and let her expertise sort through the possible whys.

Now time for treatment. She leaves the room and I undress and lie down on the table under the sheets. I've had acupuncture before and the needles don't scare or bother me. The last acupuncturist I went to also treated my boyfriend at the time and subtly commented on his pain tolerance being quite a bit lower than mine.

When Alexis returns she has a treatment plan. She goes to palpate the spot where she will put the needle in to get exactly the right point, but something odd happens. As soon as my body senses her hands coming near, the muscles involuntarily retract, trying to escape being touched. This has never happened before. I imagine her thinking I am afraid of needles and just unwilling to admit it. But I'm not, I don't know what's happening. Clearly, I don't really have anywhere to escape to, so she manages to get the needle in. My whole body tenses up. Some of the subsequent needles are painful, and with each one my body jumps in what feels like a dramatic overreaction. While Alexis makes no comment, I'm embarrassed about what a wimp I am.

When she's finished putting in the needles, she tells me she is going to leave the room to let me "rest" with them for awhile. I don't want her to leave! I'm petrified that if I move the tiniest little bit all the needles will fire up and who knows what then. I feel like a scared little porcupine. I'm too sheepish to ask her to stay, so I let her leave, though my mind is racing, my body rigid. My attempts at relaxation techniques do no good. Physical ease has apparently vanished from my body's vocabulary. When my mind tells me to relax, my body responds with *concept not found*. Even during the body work that Alexis accompanies each treatment with, the edginess remains.

Research

I have six weeks between my initial surgeon visit and the appointment with the second surgeon, so I'm trying to learn all the information I possibly can about the condition I have. When you search the internet for hip dysplasia, 9 out of 10 pages are about infants or dogs. It's much more difficult to find information on adult hip dysplasia because it is very rare. I can only spend about 15 minutes on any website before the shock reaction sets in, my hands tremble, and I start feeling dizzy. With this limiting my ability to do my own research, I have recruited as much help as I can. My mom thoroughly reads every website she can find and recaps the info, which seems somehow more palatable coming from her. I also talked to my aunt who was a nurse, another aunt who had recent experience navigating the medical system, and a cousin who did her residency at OHSU. Beyond it logistically being a good idea to have a research team and support group of trusted loved ones, I feel it's going to be essential for me to rely on their judgement. The heavy emotional cloud constantly hovering over my head makes it too scary to rely on my own judgement and ability to make decisions.

Every day I cry as I drive to teach class. Over and over my inner dialogue repeats, *How will I get through this? I have nothing to offer. I don't have the energy to give.* Once in the parking lot, I pull myself together, dry my eyes, walk into class, and teach as I always have. As soon as I am back in my car my eyes dissolve into more tears, my inner dialogue changing to, *This is all going to be taken away from me. Then what's left? I've worked too hard to get here, this is my whole life. What will be left? What will be left?* The same scene usually occurs hours later as I drive to rehearsal.

The six weeks are drawing to a close and I know the denial phase is about to be over. Soon, I will have to officially face the biggest decision I have ever made about my future.

Emily Annette Running

The only way to maintain my sanity is to feel as prepared as possible to get the answers I need.

Kickstand

I pick Mom up from the airport. She has always been my master of organizing and logical thinking, and right now that's exactly what I need. She has flown in from Montana to go to my second appointment with me. It never occurred to me to bring a guest to my appointments until a friend told me she always took someone with her. Now that I think about it, it's positively essential. I'm not one to blindly trust someone else's plan for my body without having a very good understanding of it, and it's virtually impossible to learn new information, ask pertinent questions, and then retain it all without an assistant. What a brilliant idea to have someone there taking minutes.

My mom actually insisted on coming, though I happily agreed. Not only did she want to hear the info first hand so she could work with actual information, versus my lost and emotional retelling of it, but I also sensed she felt slightly helpless being so far away. Being my mother, she has watched my progression toward a career in dance, listened to me reason out each decision I made about where to live or what job to take. She has been delighted with my successes and sympathetic to my failures. But there are just some things that a mother's love can't fix and a malformed joint structure is one of them.

When I see her I know she is just as nervous as me and I just hope that I can hold it together and show her that I'll be ok.

In preparation for my appointment the following day, we sit down at the kitchen table and write out all our questions. What are the details of the actual procedure? How long will the recovery be? Will I have limitations even after I'm healed? What is the timeline, can I put it off, or will I cause more damage if I do? Is it one hip or both hips? How common is this? Where do we find more information? Does the doctor understand that 75 percent of my income is related to my physical ability and that this surgery creates a strong conflict with my livelihood?

Inkling of clarity

<u>Journal Entry - February 28th, 2011</u>
It was a long day but not nearly as emotional as I expected. It was the day of my appointment with the surgeon who I hoped would finally give me all the answers. Of course the expectation that I would get all the answers is wildly off, but at least I have arrived at a place where I feel confident and decided about what needs to happen. I need surgery. The good news is, it's only on one hip and there is a good potential for me to return to a high level of activity. If left untreated not only would I remain in pain, but would almost inevitably be doomed to a total hip replacement within the next 10 years. Reminder: I'm 29!! and replacements need to be replaced every 10-15 years though can only be replaced twice before there's nothing left to work with! While I'm terrified of giving up my physicality, especially now when I feel at a peak, it's much better than the alternative.

There it is. The glimmer of hope that we have finally identified the cause of the problem, and there is indeed a solution. Previously, I had felt like I was looking out at a night sky, the kind far from the city where no other light dulls the thickness of black. The blackness appeared to have swallowed all the stars. In this moment, a single star's light pierced through, reminding me that the universe doesn't always reveal its intention, and sometimes we have to trust things we can't see. I can't see what this all means for my future, and where this will take me, but I can finally see my next necessary progression.

Back at my house, Mom and I sit side by side going over all the notes she took at the appointment. This time, it's she who is lost and confused with too much information and not a lot of trust in the doctor. But for me, I have turned a corner. Through Pilates, yoga, and dancing, I have studied anatomy and gone to the cadaver lab to see how our bodies are composed. By teaching and working with people's bodies, I have gained a deep understanding of how the muscles and the skeleton work together. The most important piece of information, which I finally came to terms with at this appointment, is that I am dealing with a skeletal problem, and no amount of physical therapy, acupuncture, chiropractic, rolfing, or other treatment will solve the root of the problem. The fact that I need surgery has finally clicked. After years of mystery, years of pain, years of being lost on a solution, and my current state of not being able to progress in my profession, I finally have an outline of the path necessary to make it to the next level, regardless of which direction it takes me.

The path is messy, and Mom and I spend hours looking through websites about the procedure, reading stories about the recovery, discussing a potential time-line, and going over my insurance policy.

<u>Journal Entry - March 16th, 2011</u>
I have so many little things bothering me right now, but have a feeling that they all have a similar root of unsettledness and confusion about my identity and fear of my unknown future.

Part Three

Thick blackness

I'm a walking zombie. I don't understand. How did life, or fate, or whatever is in control of it, allow me to set myself up for failure like this? As an artist, I've been specifically aware of not "putting all my eggs in one basket." All along I've reminded myself not to expect to rely on my art or my dancing to be my entire income. Expand it, have a backup plan, be prepared to fill in the gap. So I did.

I have a bachelor's degree in dance (read: movement), and between all my additional certifications and continuing education, you could say I have the equivalent of an advanced degree in "movement." I created an entire program for AWOL that allows me to combine my dancing with education. It also facilitates the growth of a nonprofit that I care about deeply, because it offers me the opportunity to perform. I have certifications in both Pilates and yoga. Since college, I've never had less than three jobs at once. My schedule has always consisted of both dancing and teaching in a variety of locations. This allows my income to draw from multiple places. Upon moving to Portland, I had set goals, both financial and career related, and I just recently achieved them all. I am at a place where I am getting paid to do what I love. I figured it out. I beat the system!

But here I am, facing losing it all in one fell swoop because from the lens I currently need to look through, all my eggs are in one basket. The physical basket. People are always saying that things happen for a reason. What is the reason? What will become clear to me in the end? The end, the end...this risky, complicated, unknown end. I can't see through the blackness because I will never know how this will turn out until I've lived through it.

This unsettledness, fear of the unknown, struggling with what is real and what is perceived, is an ongoing play between my mind and body moving at different speeds and sometimes in different directions. This chaos reminds me, I have a tool to help me handle this. Isn't that what yoga is all about? Isn't the practice of yoga meant to condition our brains and bodies to stay calm amidst chaos? I've always had an appreciation for the idea, but have never before had to put it to work to this degree. Maybe my physical knowledge and ability will be what saves me, allows me to move through this, strengthening my chances to heal. Maybe all of this will keep me conscious of the preciousness of my physicality, maybe it will also make me a better teacher.

Speaking of being a teacher, I have to tell my students. There's no way to go through this without them knowing.

Raw, exposed

The first class I talk to is my yoga class at Adidas. I always begin the class by leading the students to a comfortable seated position and brining awareness in to the breath. As everyone in class arrives on their mats, the trembling in my body returns. Instead of instructing them to close their eyes and breathe, I say I need to make an announcement. Tears are trickling out of my eyes and my voice is shaky. The tone in the room shifts as they listen silently and intently.

I tell them that I've been dealing with mysterious pain in my hip for a number of years, it has finally been diagnosed as hip dysplasia, and I will be going through major surgery in the near future to fix it. This will mean I'll be leaving Adidas at least during the recovery process, though I'm not sure what my ultimate capability will be so do not know if I'll be back, and will not know until it's happened. I try to keep it brief. Then look out at the class and realize that I'm not the only one with tears.

I proceed to teach, offering a theme for class of working with uncertainty and discomfort. I vary the length they hold each pose, and don't disclose the number of repetitions. I remind them each time to be a nonjudgmental witness to their reaction, to not knowing, and the temptation to exist beyond the moment versus right inside of it, discomfort and all. It's at that point I realize that this is when I'll reveal whether I'm a fraud. Do I practice what I teach? Am I actually qualified to be a true yoga *teacher*, or am I just skilled at performing the movements? But this class feels like one of the most genuine I've ever taught. The concepts that we explore in yoga now so directly applicable to everything I am navigating.

The great challenge is not to disintegrate into a mush of depression and hide away from the world, hoping it will all go away. Many times I wish I could do exactly that. Instead I have been compelled to go through this experience very openly. I want to show that it's okay to accept sadness, and not escape from it, or mask it with polite insincerity. I want to reveal vulnerability in its most raw form as a reminder that we are all human and deserve compassion. This will inevitably require me to expose my weaknesses, set aside my ego, and acknowledge my physical limitations despite my physical abilities being what I consider my greatest talent.

***

A few days later, I am teaching the advanced level aerial class at AWOL. For most of the students I was their first teacher and have been with them through their entire progression. As the founder of the education program, I have been the person they come to for everything. At the end of class, I gather everyone around. This time, the struggle to maintain my composure is much more difficult. This is the part of my life I've worked the hardest for, and these are the students that have made the education program, that I spent years creating, successful. I don't even know what to say. I don't know how to tell them. My throat constricts, and I choke on my words, as I try to summarize. My students are crying with me before I even get it out. Not realizing I've been dealing with pain for years, they are completely blindsided by the thought that my body isn't performing well. Of all people, they understand how much this means to me, and it appears that my broken heart has broken their hearts too. I am touched beyond measure at their concern, and their compassion is what gives me strength to keep moving forward with surgery.

Overwhelming gibberish

I'm on hold with aggravating music that sounds like it's streaming from another century, occasionally interrupted by a recording telling me how valuable my call is. I've never had a job with benefits, and I pay for insurance out of my own pocket. This is the first claim I've ever made, and there's a lot I am unfamiliar with. It doesn't help that the procedure I'm trying to learn about is rare and considered elective. But when I try to learn the language and understand my options, it feels more like a big sea of overwhelming gibberish intended to confuse me into defeat. The insurance system itself is an enormous part of the problem and widely known to be broken. Still, early in the process I've come to realize I am my only advocate.

Finally, a person on the other end of the line. Inevitably, a different person than I spoke with last time, so I recap my story for the millionth time. Their tone is sterile, but their language is intended to seem helpful. I am not fooled. I've prepared for the call, have my questions written out, my notes from the previous call (a mere few days ago), in front of me. With my logic carefully reasoned out, I just might be able to ask the right question that will trick them into guiding me in the right direction. Already 15 minutes in, and we are still sorting through the same material I went over in the last call. My frustration is building. I feel like Alice from Alice in Wonderland. With each question, I am genuinely trying to understand what to do and make sense of the world around me, yet each answer feels like a contrary riddle confusing me even more. It is one thing not to already know how to navigate the insurance system, but to be unable to find out from people who are supposed to provide me with information is unacceptable.

The frustration finally breaks, I'm sobbing and pleading with the person on the other end of the line to have compassion. To understand where I'm coming from. I say, "I don't mean to shoot the messenger, but you are the only one I have access to." The emotion is pouring out and I can't stop it, but I also get lost in it. I'm helpless. Why am I helpless? How is it possible to feel so helpless?

Amidst endless dialogue, and many unsuccessful calls to my insurance company, there is the rare occurrence when the logic and the compassion meet up, and the person at the other end of the line gives me one little tidbit. One piece of the puzzle that leads me to the essential next step, dawning a sliver of hope that if I keep pushing forward they may eventually cave in before me, and I will actually receive health coverage.

Simultaneously, I've also been talking to OHSU as I applied, and have been approved, for financial assistance. A big part of why I put off discovering what was really going on in my body was financial. It meant the possibility of throwing away thousands of dollars to come out empty handed, when no one, doctor or otherwise, had been able to convince me they had a good idea of what was causing my pain. While I have been approved for financial assistance, I am still unsure of what exactly it entails and keep getting passed from person to person in my pursuit of understanding.

More questions

March 28, 2011

Today is my second appointment with Dr. Holt. My aunt Louisa has driven up from Eugene to go with me, and we have quite the agenda for the day. While I've made a valiant attempt to understand how insurance benefits are handled, and procedural eligibility works with financial assistance, there is still no direct answer. The latter has something to do with the diagnostic code for my procedure and whether it is considered above or below the line in regards to the Oregon Health Plan's list of priorities. Huh?

First, we call Liza with OHSU Financial Assistance. She breaks down the criteria for approval (though I'm already approved), and renewal process, as assistance is only valid for six months at a time. The lingering question is if the financial assistance will cover my exact procedure. I've been told, though I have no idea who told me at this point, that approval is somehow dependent on prior-authorization from insurance. For this we must speak with Jean.

Jean is the surgery scheduler at Dr. Holt's office, as well as the one in charge of gaining prior-authorization for surgeries. Her office is in the same building as my appointment so I arrange to meet her in person right before I see Dr. Holt. Louisa and I discuss the "get to the point" list of things I need to know. I feel much better having a witness to the conversation to ensure I'm not misunderstanding or overlooking key details.

I ask Jean about how the process from scheduling to surgery goes including prior-authorization and billing of insurance.

Notes from the conversation:
She and Molly are the coordinators of benefits between OHSU and insurance. All bills are submitted to my insurance company so that

they can be added to the deductible amount. They will get pre-authorization prior to any surgical procedure. They will notify me of any glitches that may arise.

I ask what is the status of my financial assistance.

The diagnostic and procedural codes do not come under the approval of Oregon Health Plan therefore they are not approved for the OHSU plan. Jean has submitted my request to the OHSU Review Board where a doctor decides if they will make an exception and cover it. This doc will most likely ask Dr. Holt for his notes and input. She is not sure when they will make a decision.

I ask how it works if I decide to move forward.

If I decide to go ahead with surgery following my appointment today, it could be scheduled as early as April or May.

Onward we go to speak with Dr. Holt. Despite the emotional turning point following my first appointment, I have a new list of questions before I will decide whether to move forward with the surgery. One thing my previous appointment lacked was an official recommendation of what to do.

Dr. Holt continues to surprise me with his patience. After each answer he pauses to make sure I am satisfied with the response. He listens, and does not make me feel rushed. He does not seem bothered when I ask him to explain many of the same things over again.

<u>Louisa's notes from the appointment:</u>
I ask specifics about the procedure.

He explains (using less harsh terms than the first surgeon), *he will cut the bone in three places, freeing it up, and then moving it to the correct position.*

I ask how they will determine the placement.

He describes that *x-rays taken the day of surgery will determine the placement, with the goal being achieving the best possible placement for stability. The incision is a "pocket cut" in a curve around the area where your front pocket would be on a pair of pants. He will use screws to hold the bone in place. Six months post surgery they can be removed in a simple day procedure. As for the labral tear, he will not know how to proceed until he is in there and can see what is going on. Hopefully, it will be intact enough that he can use suture anchors to attach it back in place.*

I ask how long the surgery will take.

The surgery will be scheduled to take six hours, though he doesn't expect it to take that long, he just wants to assure that nothing else gets scheduled that day. Dr. Rossman, who is a hip trauma specialist, will assist him due to the technical difficulty of the surgery.

I ask what are the specific risks of surgery.

-The bones not healing is a risk, though unlikely based on my excellent health.
-Infection (also low chance due to good health).
-Blood loss, 50 percent chance of a transfusion during procedure.
-This is a technically difficult surgery, so few doctors do it. He does 3-4 per year. Usually the person has more severe dysplasia, with lower expectations for outcome. Mine is mild dysplasia and thus has the best chance for a positive outcome.

Finally I ask, what do you recommend?

He breaks down my options.

Option 1: Do nothing, no surgery of any kind, and continue on physically as usual.

Result: guaranteed a total hip replacement within 10 years, maybe sooner, determined by mechanical factors and bio-chemical markers. Post replacement would require living with restrictions of hip movements.

Option 2: Do nothing, no surgery of any kind, and reduce all physical activity to a minimum.

Result: potentially delay total hip replacement for longer, though not guaranteed. Increased risk of arthritis developing due to continued wear on the bone.

Option 3: Proceed with the Periacetabular Osteotomy, which will assist in preserving the integrity of the joint for much longer.

Result: goals here are to prevent early arthritis due to wear on the bone and decrease or eliminate pain being caused by the labral tear. Successful surgery would ideally lead to correction of the problem. Will potentially decrease range of motion of the hip, though once the bone is healed there would be no actual restrictions of movement.

All questions checked off the list, we head home. Once in the car, Louisa asks the simple question, "So, are you ready to schedule?"

Dr. Holt had just laid out my options in the most clear and concise way possible, and while the answer seems completely unquestionable, I can't respond with a distinct "yes." I am still holding tightly to the last thread of denial.

A little shocked, Louisa is acutely aware that it has to be me that makes the decision of whether to go through with it, so she gently guides me through. I stress about finances since we still have no idea what surgery would actually cost, nor if I will even have help paying for it. She acknowledges that being a consideration, but brings me back to the essential priority of body necessity. She reads from her notes the facts of what is going on in my body, and we follow the most logical and structured path towards a decision; we make a "pros and cons" list.

Pros:
OHSU is an excellent facility
Dr. Holt an excellent doctor
Attacks root of the problem
Confidence in recovery/success of procedure
No more pain
Support/help available
Financial possibilities-OHSU financial assistance/insurance

Cons:
Risks of surgery
Continue managing symptoms

The following day, I call Jean and have a surgery date set for May 6th.

Pure fear

<u>Journal Entry - April 17th, 2011</u>
Despite caring family and friends willing to support me, no one lives with the thought of what's to come every moment of every day like I do. No one can feel the weight of this decision. No one can feel the fear of being sedentary for months, especially in contrast to my current lifestyle of multiple hours of highly physical activities every day.

AWOL is in our final weeks of rehearsal leading up to "Zip Zap Doom," the sequel to the show we did this fall, "Zip Zap Zoom." It's taking exceptional effort to release the thought that this could be my last performance as a dancer. Surgery this major has many risks and I am trying to prepare for whatever my future will be. You know how sometimes when a person in your life dies, and you say, I wish I would have spoken to them more, or done things differently when I had the chance. Well, it's like that, I feel like I might as well live out my performance as if it might be my last so I won't look back and wish I had done it differently. I want to work hard and do my best, focusing on the enjoyment I get from performing rather than the pain and fear of the future.

The main apparatus I am working on is the spanish web, which looks strikingly similar to a simple rope. In the piece, my character (Zap) does physical training with the Ninja who has been overshadowed by the Unicorn as "favorite pet," and is trying to regain her status. The piece is intense, and begins with me dropping from the ceiling in a move called the "star fall." I climb up to the top of the rope in the dark... wrap in, invert, hook my right knee, wrap the rope once around my left leg and then twice around my waist. The Ninja opens the piece with a warm-up dance and on the musical cue, she points at me and I open into a spread eagle star shape and unwind until the rope cinches around my leg. That's my bad side, but my grimace isn't noticeable because I'm supposed to be a badass and I can easily pass it off as a villainous look of challenge at the Ninja. Now we begin a long unison sequence of climbs, inverts, one arm spin, one knee hang...in the final section I do a "spider climb," which means I'm climbing feet first, 20 feet up to a hand loop. I wrap in my wrist, pull the safety keeper down tight, and prepare for the "death spin." Dangling by one arm, my partner on the floor spins the rope so fast that my body is nearly horizontal to the ground. This is again where my trust issues arise. Not with my partner, not with the rigging, but with myself and my own strength and ability. Fear surging through my veins, and my mind spiraling off to nowhere, my body completes the task exactly as it knows how, and the piece is over. Two weekends in a row, six shows total, the same mental struggle occurs every time.

The what-ifs

<u>Journal Entry - April 20th, 2011</u>
I'm so scared. While the pain is unbearable, making the surgery feel like a potential fix, the pain has also been taking on a new form, making me nervous that this isn't the end. The deep, sharp groin pain that I've only ever felt on my left side is now coming up on my right as well. I don't know what that means. I know I have a labral tear on both sides, but the hip dysplasia is only a concern on the left. I can't shake the fear that I have a lifetime of hip problems ahead of me. I am also scared that I won't be able to return to what I'm doing now. I'm scared of losing the people that currently surround me. I'm scared that I'll never be financially secure. I'm scared knowing my independence will inevitably need to be surrendered. I'm scared that all these insecurities building up are going to push people away from me.

With just a few weeks to go until the procedure, the world around me seems surreal. I have become distinctly attuned to all of the things I take for granted. I have become aware of every set of stairs that I bound up with ease on a daily basis...stairs to get in the house, stairs to my room, stairs to do laundry, stairs at work. Every time I demonstrate a movement in class, I remind myself that 29 years of training my muscles went into my abilities, and I wonder how long it will take to get back. I notice old people, and wonder what it's like to feel like them. I notice handicapped people, and consider what circumstance got them there. I'm trying to make sense of the bigger picture. I'm trying to visualize how the things I identify with may shift, and what those possibilities could look like.

In many ways I have already become a stranger to myself. The strength of emotions are more overpowering than I thought possible, stripping me of the carefree, cheerful, silly person most people knew me as, and leaving me this haunt of a person depleted by the fluctuations of grief.

Removing the last strip of the mask

I am desperate for insight and wisdom and something to ease my mind. I am in the thick of it, and need to consult with someone who has been there, can relate, yet is past it and onto their future. Cousin Kesa.

Kesa was home-schooled so she could focus her attention on ballet. Classical ballet. Then she grew to be 5'9," and her long, beautiful, graceful body no longer fit the classic ballerina mold, and she had to work twice as hard as the rest to establish her place. Chosen to apprentice for a prestigious ballet company, she seized the opportunity to display her abilities. Her heart full of hope, and her mind utterly focused, she worked so hard that she caused stress fractures in both her legs. This forced her to take time off and re-evaluate the role of dance in her life.

Journal Entry - May 1st, 2011
Cousin Kesa brought to my attention a unique element contributing to how I'm dealing with it all, which is the dancer in me. After finishing a six show run, requiring intense physical strength, one of my students came to me and said, 'I watched you so intently during the show to see if I could detect any grimace of pain or faltering and came to the conclusion: how could Emily's body, THAT body, possibly need surgery!!" That comment struck a chord that initiated my last hoorah of doubt. The intensity of the surgery felt incongruent to the capability my body still possessed. Kesa wisely reminded me that dancers are a unique breed who are trained to take what is challenging and painful and make it look easy. We cultivate the ability to have ease and lightness in our bodies, and in the expression on our face, when underneath, we could have bloody toes, broken bones, or dysplastic hips. While as an artist and performer I am encouraged to feel the depth of my emotions, the dancer in me expects any falter to be masked.

I feel ultimately consoled knowing that doing my best and being open to the outcome is the only way to proceed. Since there's no possible way to know how all the "what ifs" will pan out, there is no need or benefit to forcing resolve. Once again, I return to the serenity prayer, and hope I can know the difference between changing that which can be changed and letting go of the rest.

Preparing for hibernation

Two weeks to go before surgery and there's an overwhelming amount of things to prepare for. First, my mom will be coming to be with me at the hospital and then help me during the initial few weeks when there are many things I won't be able to do for myself. I will be unable to bear weight on my left leg for six to eight weeks, which means I will be on a walker or crutches. I also may need a raised toilet seat so my hip doesn't bend beyond the acceptable angle. We plan to purchase those items before leaving the hospital, but will wait until we really know what I need. We will also be staying at my mom's sisters house who lives in town. The sad truth of it is, I will probably need constant care for at least an additional week after leaving the hospital. I just can't seem to picture it though. I've never had so much as a sprained ankle slow me down so this will be an extreme transition from being so physically independent. I haven't come to terms with the fact that I will need someone to help me shower, cook, grocery shop, get in and out of the car, etc., but I am grateful that I have family who are willing and able to help.

Once I move back to my house, I will also need to make some adjustments. As part of the pre-op appointments the doctors make sure you have appropriate accommodations for your restrictions. My bedroom is currently on the second floor, so I will not be able to get to it for two months. Luckily, one of my housemates has agreed to switch with me temporarily. I've been trying to make a mental inventory of all the things I will need to pack to get me through the first couple weeks, and once I'm home as well. In addition to packing the clothing I will need, I plan to bring my desk and file cabinet downstairs. If I'm going to be forced to lay around, I suppose it's a good time to do things no one ever has time nor desire to do, like clean out my hard drive and organize my filing.

While I will have my mom around, my students and friends have also very graciously offered to organize a schedule of meal deliveries for me, if I need. Though my initial reaction to accepting help feels more like resistance, I am working on changing my perspective to focus on both the generosity of the gesture, as well as the fact it may be a necessity. I don't know what it is about asking for help that feels so uncomfortable. Regardless, until I know what recovery really looks like, I've avoided officially putting the meal delivery schedule together. Hopefully, the offer of assistance will make it easier to ask for if the time comes.

Wrapping up loose ends

Since I won't even be walking for six to eight weeks, I have given up all my work. My last day will be May 5th - I refuse to give anything up any sooner than is necessary. Currently, I'm teaching 15 classes a week. I imagine that even with best case scenario, I will probably be away from teaching aerial the longest since it's the most intense, and nearly impossible to teach without the ability to demonstrate. My students promise me that they would love to take my class even if I had to be on crutches, but really, that only works in theory. So I've given up the aerial classes more permanently, and if, or when the time comes, I hope that they can find a new place for me on the schedule.

My Adidas Pilates and yoga classes have been making similarly desperate requests. They suggested having me skype teach them from bed, or recording all my classes leading up to my absence, which they would replay back instead of having a new teacher! Of course, the healing process requires extensive rest and I plan to commit to it as best I can. I do not want to jeopardize the outcome.

For the past few months, if I hadn't been reliant on the income of teaching as well as the support from all my students, I probably wouldn't have wanted to get out of bed.

Part Four

What happened?

Journal Entry - May 5th, 2011
Today marks the first day of yet a new chapter. Surgery was supposed to happen tomorrow, but has been postponed due to insurance complications. Our health care system has failed me for now and is trying to avoid giving me coverage. After moving at a million miles an hour toward surgery, I am now neither recovering nor working. I had to give up all my work to plan for the two months that I would be immobile. At this point, I am trying to take a step back and plan my next moves carefully. What I know is that for short-term, maintaining the level of physicality I was working with is not possible. What I also know is despite not having surgery now, I will have it in the future, so choosing to relieve my income from being dependent on my body is essential. While it's a huge disappointment to build up to something that falls through at the last minute, I'm trying to look at all the benefits that could come of this. I will get to have a summer and enjoy it without crutches. I will be able to work my way into a better financial position before going through with it, and hopefully have more security on the other end.

Yet, while those are hugely positive things, I'm nervous about it all falling into place. As usual, my impatience and urgency are getting in the way. I am trying hard to be calm and give myself time, but underneath, all I want is any small shred of security to hold on to.

Late yesterday afternoon I canceled the upcoming surgery, or maybe better put, postponed it until more information can be obtained. It has been a strenuous few months trying to deal with OHSU and my insurance company. Along the way I have received misinformation, conflicting information, and wrong information, as the gigantic maze of people I'm told to call keep passing me on to someone else who passes me on to someone else.

At this point my individual insurance has stalled the process and has not agreed to authorize the surgery. I thought they were reviewing for medical necessity, but I have also learned there is more.

Apparently, my insurance policy has something called a '24 month unlisted clause.' *Unlisted? As in I am not allowed to be aware of it?* What does the 24 month unlisted clause say? It allegedly states that within the first two years of my policy, for me ending July 1st, 2011, they can review my claims to assure there are not conditions I previously had that weren't acknowledged on my initial application. They will do this by contacting every doctor I've seen within the past five years to see if I have ever brought this issue up, and if I did, they will drop my policy due to fraud. I am still unsure as to whether an official diagnosis is necessary for them to drop me, or if it could be as minimal as a note on my chart.

The facts are that I have had this since birth, but wasn't diagnosed until months ago. Yes, I have known about it due to pain, but did not include random pain that happens sporadically which no doctor can identify the cause of, on my insurance application. If they do drop my policy they will also demand reimbursement for any money they have spent on me and reimburse me for all the premiums I've paid. In the end, regardless of how the math evens out, I will be without insurance, and without potential to qualify for any other. This is potentially very, very bad news.

The second crack in the windshield

The first crack in the windshield, the diagnosis, spanned across the bottom of the windshield from one side clear across to the other. Though not completely blocking my vision, it glared back at me every time I looked forward. When surgery fell through I had already been driving down a narrow canyon road, rock cliff straight to the sky on the passenger's side, rock cliff straight over the edge on the driver's side. Then one renegade rock broke loose from the wall, tumbling down at a velocity faster than allowed me to react, skipping across the windshield, adding a vertical crack lining up equidistance between my two eyes. Looking straight ahead made me cross-eyed, so I had to lean a little to the left or a little to the right to get a view of the road. With each additional crack a windshield becomes more fragile such that the next pebble - it doesn't take more than a pebble - that hits it causes the break to spread out like a spider web until finally it just shatters.

<u>Journal Entry - May 12th, 2011</u>
I'm on my way down to Tucson to visit my sister and decompress. The past few months have taken a big toll and I'm feeling lost and scared about the future. It is essential for me to find some distance from it all and clear my head.

I feel in a complete state of freefall. My career and financial future is shaky. My physical future is unknown. I'm losing confidence in my ability to face this. Of course, I can and I will, but I can't seem to come to a place of acceptance with being in such a dark place. Going to read and re-read Pema Chodron's "Wisdom of No Escape," until I find the ability and skills to keep peace of mind. There is no escape from this, only my ability to shape my perspective.

Redefinition

For as long as I can remember I've been of the mindset that if I wanted to pursue dancing I had better get to it, because at 20 you're terrified that by 30 you'll be considered geriatric in the field! Well, I'm 29, and though not officially geriatric, I am dealing with hip issues and facing major hip surgery so I guess my circumstance substantiates some of those fears! On the other hand, at 29 I have come to feel more knowledgeable, more mature, and better at what I do than when I was 20. I also have evolved to realize that while some aspects of my dance career may need to retire earlier than others, I still have at least another decade to go before that occurs.

So, how do I fit it all in? I need to get this surgery pushed through. Then what if I need to go through the process again with the other hip? Well, that takes a couple years out of the decade. And then what about kids? Yep, I want to have kids someday, and approaching my 30's they tell me that is supposed to happen sooner rather than later. Subtract another year or two from that decade. But wait, I'm not even in a relationship, and how will I have time for that when clearly I'm such a mess of a person myself that I'll never meet anyone until I emerge from this. Hmmm, so much to consider, time to redefine.

Since my physical future is unknown anyway, let's start with how this will affect my profession. I can be okay with the thought that this is setting me up for more success in the future. It's much safer not to have my entire income dependent on extreme physicality even if I can come back to that on some level. While I wouldn't have chosen to make that transition right now, I will accept that it's helping me move in the right direction.

So, let's take a look at my resume. Oh dear, it appears that my resume has built me up to doing exactly what I'm doing, which is what I'm now not able to do. Okay...let's take a look at my skills. Where do I start? I ask my colleague, friend and current housemate to assist. She knows me on many levels, and may have insight for me that is free from the emotional cloud I feel surrounded by. The bigger picture is so petrifying, I have no idea how I fit into it!

She helps me tally it up. I created my own business, including designing and building my own website, developing curriculum, handling finances, etc. Good, good. While working with various nonprofits, I've been required to wear many hats, so I can speak to Education, Community Outreach, Development, Marketing, Class Management, and Program Development. Okay, starting to look more encouraging. I've been involved in multiple industries, Nonprofit Arts, Health and Fitness, and Production. True. Unfolding this list into my new resume, I am ready to put it to the test! As for my personal life, I'll have to address that later.

<u>Journal Entry - May 19th, 2011</u>
My heart is suffocating. My physicality is deteriorating. I'm beyond overwhelmed. My entire career so far has been dedicated to learning about, practicing, and experiencing the mind/body connection. My mind is on track, but my body isn't keeping up. I don't know how to keep my soul alive without dance, yoga, and the ability to express myself physically. This is where the pain and restlessness become unbearable. I don't know how to follow my heart anymore because it's lost in a dark room. My emotions are stifled from the requirement to plow forward. My body is suffering. My mind is exhausted. I have many people to support my decision, but few to guide me. I long for guidance. Life is full of so many things beyond our power, control, dictation. We are vulnerable whether or not we realize it. When that fact becomes illuminated, it's a very potent discovery.

My heart went out to you

I'm back in my primary physician's office where it all began. I don't know what to do with my body between now and when my surgery will actually occur, so I decided to consult with Dr. Keating, as he's a sports medicine physician and will understand my goals. My biggest concern is making things worse by continuing to do high performance activities. I'm hoping he will be able to advise me on what is safe and what I should avoid, while also helping me find ways to remain active.

When he walks in the room and the first words out of his mouth are, "My heart went out to you when I saw the results of the MRI. You have been through so much in the past few months. What can I do for you today?" I'm startled by his compassion and immediately feel more at ease. He understands my need to continue to be active, and we discuss what causes my pain and the potential consequences of ignoring it. He suggests kayaking, swimming, or other such activities that avoid inducing more stress and wear on the hip joint. He reminds me that the hardest part will be that I have to *choose* to pull back, whereas surgery would have forced me to take it easy. It is important that I don't push that boundary.

The portion of the conversation I came for is closing when he brings up one more thing. He very directly asks if I've been experiencing any depression. *Are you kidding? I'm a wreck, a disaster, a lunatic!* I think to myself. But depression isn't something someone like me should have. I'm happy, optimistic, idealistic and strong, this is just a moment. I respond out loud with a timid, "Yes, a little." With a compassionate tone and direct words he describes to me that the sudden decrease in physical activity alone would cause depression due to the dramatic decrease in serotonin, a chemical the brain naturally produces during exercise. He assures me every athlete dealing with injury goes through this and he would be happy to find me the right prescription if I decide I need it.

Journal Entry - June 5th, 2011

I talked to my acupuncturist recently about depression because I've been feeling a sadness that seems to be rooted deep into the core of my being. I've never felt sadness like this before. The quickness and intensity at which it can arise. Crying at small things and crying shamelessly in public. I've lost confidence. I've lost hope and trust. It's truly a state of fragility I've never experienced before. My doctor had brought it up previously, and I'm lucky he brought it up because as a generally happy, optimistic, idealistic, and supposedly strong individual, it's hard to admit to yourself, let alone others, that you could ever experience clinical depression. Still, I'm not super excited about medication, so I consulted my acupuncturist first. She completely agreed with the doc and encouraged me to closely monitor how I was doing. Though in Eastern medicine there is no "depression pill," so she inquired very thoroughly about other emotions and/or body functions that could be related, and recommended a special formula of Chinese herbs. Also she suggested 5HTP which I am so grateful for! It's an african root which serves as a neurotransmitter support, and made a profound difference. I was literally able to feel lightness again when previously I felt surrounded by thick blackness.

Identity without affiliations

I gave up all my jobs for surgery and, while the procedure didn't happen, I don't feel right taking them back. It would be unfair to the people who stepped up to cover me, and in reality, I know that I will have to give them up again in the near future. I am making the decision to focus my attention on forward motion instead.

What I have discovered, though, is how much we rely on our affiliations to define our identity. Now that I'm not dancing or teaching or working, I absolutely dread the elevator because my speech is empty! Okay, I rarely ride on elevators, but my point is that my current set of circumstances changes how I meet new people and interact in new social situations. Our society is built to ask, "What do you do?" as an initial means to getting to know someone. But I have no answer, so what does that mean? If I say I'm in transition they want to know why, but it's too emotional to talk about my past, yet I have no idea what to say about my future. If I confess I'm searching for a job people try to be helpful and ask idiotic things like "Have you looked on Craigslist?" Just because I'm jobless doesn't mean I'm incompetent! While I know they are well meaning, it's not a conversation I enjoy having and I'm often left feeling defeated and unable to connect with the world.

There have been many people in my life who have told me that they have no doubt that whatever I set my mind to, I will succeed. While I've felt like an immense failure on many occasions, their confidence has stuck with me. Maybe I will have to change my profession. I wonder if it's possible that there's something else out there that I'm good at and just as passionate about, but haven't discovered yet. I wonder what it will feel like if everything I've known up until now changes.

Gut alien

The bathroom floor is cold and dirty, though that feels quite irrelevant to me despite that I'm lying here again in the middle of the night. Tears stream out of the corner of my eyes and I'm prodding at my abdomen. The pain is not even related to my hip. It occurs right where the ribcage ends and the soft, vulnerable middle begins. Pain is the wrong word. Nausea is the wrong word. But it's somewhere in between. It feels heavy and dark, swimming and churning. It's so tangible I feel if I could just reach inside I could pull it out and then it would be gone. Like a little alien took up residence in my gut. Oh, how I wish he would emerge. I'm in the bathroom because I'm trying to throw him up. He wakes me in the middle of the night squirming away in there and I lie squirming in bed until he also takes over my brain and I have no awareness of anything else except a focused mission to get it out, make the feeling lift. Finally, I throw up four times, though nothing really comes out. I crawl back to bed, weak and shivering.

Unexpected triumph

Tuesday June 7th, 2011

Since my original surgery date of May 6th fell through, I have recruited help from my aunt Lulu, who is a public health nurse in Oregon, to help me determine how to proceed.

Aunt Lulu talked to people she knew and came up with a few backup options in the case my insurance rejects authorization of surgery entirely. She spoke with someone from the Health Advocacy Bureau and he told her it would be best to file an appeal. He listed the items I should incorporate in my appeal including the doctor's recommendation, arguments on medical necessity, and the cost effective analysis of the Periacetabular Osteotomy now, versus a Total Hip Replacement in a few years.

The last time I spoke with insurance, I first asked what it would take to get authorization pushed through now that this unexpected pre-existing condition investigation was added to the requirements for approval. The person I spoke with told me that they absolutely would not proceed until they received the medical records they requested from my gynecologist. I have specifically avoided releasing those records (which require appearing in person to sign off) since learning about the 24 month unlisted clause which may allow my insurance to drop my policy. I am currently bordering on that 24 month deadline and have been attempting to get more information before making a decision to risk losing my policy for the sake of getting authorization sooner. This feels like the one piece of the puzzle I have some control of.

The second portion of this conversation I brought up my backup plan to appeal if necessary, asking very directly if I had the facts straight for what I would do if it came to that and confirming the materials I would need to submit. The information provided was unclear and incomplete.

Today I have a conference call scheduled with a woman from insurance and my mom. When I scheduled the call I requested to have a witness involved in the conversation to help me take notes and ingest all the information. Despite taking notes as best I can, each conversation seems to leave many questions unanswered. At the scheduled time, I call in and the woman I am speaking with says, "Let's just pull up your account first and check in on the status..." *Fine*, I thought, *but you're not going to find anything new because you told me very directly last time that there was no possible way you would approve it with out my records.*

There is a pause on the other end of the line until she blithely states, "okay, so it looks like you're approved for surgery, any other questions?"

Huh?? Excuse me? Could you say that again? And can you tell me what the F#% changed??*

I am so dumbfounded I don't even know what to say. What happened to the fraud case and how am I suddenly and miraculously approved?

After a short consideration of the circumstance, I realize this is a prime example of when it's best to let the past be the past and I don't question the hows or the whys further. Instead, I leap right into inquiries about the future. When can I schedule? What are the details? How is this communicated with OHSU? Are there any other potential conflicts that may arise that I wouldn't know to ask about? I've got to get this on the books before they change their minds!

Paper panic

<u>Journal Entry - July 6th, 2011</u>
Surgery has been approved, I'm relieved about that, but alas, that's only one item on a list of items that I need to sort through. I've been without a job for two months now and am feeling nervous about when I'll have an income again. I have been going about the job search in many ways. Originally, I was just trying to get a job, any basic admin job that gave me a paycheck, and applying to as many places as possible. Unfortunately, that has been failing miserably. I don't have direct admin experience on my resume and have never actually worked in an office environment before. As you might imagine, I have zero appeal to anyone hiring for such a position. My second plan includes pursuing a more career type job which quite frankly, overwhelms me. I have very little confidence at this point, and the circumstances of my life don't leave much energy left for re-inventing myself. Regardless, my current strategy has become spending my time and effort cultivating relationships and connections with people in my field, and really just getting on their radar. This change of strategy has lead me to begin an internship with a major nonprofit. No idea how this will turn out, I'm trying to convince myself that I have a plan and that it's the best way for me to move forward. The possibility of running out of money is very real right now and it's terrifying. Even if my parents and family will help me, I just don't know how to manage the thought of not being independent.

I'm so happy or relieved or something. I have been working with one of Portland's biggest nonprofits as a volunteer and it's reminding me that I have something to offer...well kind of. Let's go back to the beginning. I have been searching for jobs, with no definite outcome yet, so scored myself a volunteer position in an office. It's challenging to work for free when my rent is in danger of not getting paid, but it has also been very helpful for me for a few reasons. For example, before I get my fancy real person job, I should probably conquer my irrational fear of offices so I don't make a fool of myself. You see, it's not like I haven't done the same type of work one would do in an office, it's just that I did it from home or my private office in AWOL's cold warehouse, and the change of setting intimidates me.

I am genuinely nervous about the silliest things, for example, I don't know what to wear. I know it's the 21st century, but is it inappropriate to have exposed shoulders in July?? While you may be mocking me, my usual work attire often includes unitards, so I dare you to imagine the tables are turned. You have a new job as a dancer and you will be walking into your first day of work in a unitard. I'm telling you that my scenario felt no different than how I imagine that would make most people feel!

I also have an irrational fear of office equipment, specifically copy machines. They never seem to work right, either getting jammed, wasting paper, or just plain being a nuisance - making the operator of them appear inept. One of my main tasks as a volunteer is taking hundreds of folders of projects and scanning them in to a digital archive.

Deep sigh, here goes. I open one folder, remove all paper clips and staples, sometimes separate them into smaller stacks depending on the number of pages, put it in the feeder select all the right locations for it to be sent to and press "go" or "start" or whatever. Scanning scanning scanning...I prepare the next folder as I wait. Awkward noise followed by process coming to an abrupt halt. Jammed, huh, typical. I maneuver the paper out of the feeder and try to continue on, though it has forgotten what it was doing, and I have to start the stack over. The majority of my time is spent at the copy machine and sometimes I have to step aside while someone else needs to use it. Minimally intensive observation convinces me that I am not the irrational one, the copier is. Fear conquered, irritation vindicated.

Then there was the computer incident. I haven't worked on a PC in years since I have a Mac. Upon scanning a stack of folders, I head back to my desk to rename the files.

My computer has fallen asleep and does not wake up to pressing keys. I see a little button with a house icon on it and feel like that probably will help bring me back to my home page so I can log in and continue my work. I press the button and crash, my computer stops working. It won't turn on or off and the screen has numericalettery gibberish on it. I get the IT guy, who fixes the problem and then cuts out a little square of pink paper, then writes an X on it and tapes it over the button I'm apparently never supposed to touch. I feel like I'm in the first grade.

    Luckily, the woman who hired me recognizes that my capacity is well beyond an intern with no work experience, and instead sends me off to shadow various employees on projects that would be more relevant to the work I'm looking for.

White Bird

Journal Entry - August 14th, 2011
It was a rough day. Actually that applies to the whole week. The good news is that I got a job! The bad news is my excitement about it feels slightly overshadowed with the reality of all the changes that are about to take place. I also really just want a good workout. My body feels awful. The pain is more under control than before but I just feel wretched and out of shape. I panicked a bit today about the thought of not getting my strength and physicality back again. It doesn't help that my 30th birthday is in a week, which is just a reminder that I'm not getting any younger. I'm lacking confidence right now and do hope it will pass soon.

    White Bird, a nonprofit that brings in dance companies from all over the world and presents them on a Portland stage, has been on my radar since I moved here. I often volunteer as an usher at their shows so I can watch the productions and work among the organization. I also was introduced to Chelsea, their Audience Services Manager, who knows my cousin and is also a dancer.

    Earlier this summer, I contacted Chelsea to feel out if there may be any upcoming opportunities to work with White Bird. She shared the potential of a development/admin position being in discussion, budget dependent. Little heart icons appear in my eyes with the thought of being able to combine my dance background with working in development for this well-regarded organization. I've been trying to think creatively of ways to give myself an upper hand if this position does eventually come to exist, or potentially a proposal for a different context in which to develop the position. So, I write a letter of interest to the two co-founders Paul and Walter, and wait for a response.

    The co-founders emphasize that there are no paid positions available, but invite me to meet with them, agreeing to talk about volunteer possibilities. I agree and meet up with them at their home office, a gorgeous house on the hill right next to OSHU. They send me to the study while they finish up a staff meeting and then come in to chat. I speak very genuinely about my intent to become more involved in the greater arts community of Portland, discuss my work with AWOL and other relevant background pieces, including my passion for remaining connected internationally. Having both lived in Paris, Paul and I are able to exchange some stories from common ground. I share how my year in Paris gave me the tools to express the value of arts in the community, and I am eager to continue my pursuit towards a stronger arts community in Portland. I very directly include that while I am looking for a part time job in development, ideally with an arts organization, I would like to specifically get involved with White Bird on any level because I think so highly of their mission.

Two weeks later, they called me and offered me a newly created development position! The truth is, their mission makes me giddy to talk about. Each season, White Bird brings in 12 of the highest quality companies from all over the world including Israel, Brazil, Sweden, France, Australia, and the U.S., exposing Portland audiences to the international stage. They have educated audiences about dance and taught them to appreciate the variety and scope of dance available. From my dancer's perspective, I also believe they have the ability to push Portland dance companies to the cutting edge by exposing us to a wide spectrum of quality work, as well as keeping the bar high.

Things are always supposed to make more sense in retrospect, and I think I get it finally. I have indeed been jobless for nearly three and a half months now, but the wait was worth it, because instead of working some random at-least-it's-a-paycheck job, I'll be working for a company with a mission that could not suit me better! While it's only part time and does not provide benefits as I had hoped, I feel confident with how it fits into the bigger picture.

Public versus private

I am so happy about my new position with White Bird, though am having a bit of an emotional dilemma. It's one where my brain and my gut aren't meeting on the same page and I don't know exactly how to handle it. Luckily, my sister is much better with logic than me, so I call her up. I describe to her that my goal is to maintain a long term role with the organization, though in the short term I know I will soon need to ask for a month off to undergo and recover from surgery. I was aware that I needed surgery when I originally spoke with them, but it didn't seem necessary to bring up considering we were discussing volunteer opportunities. Now, in retrospect my conscience is confusing me and I am concerned that I should have disclosed that information at the time.

My sister, who is getting her PhD in Sociology, recognizes the conundrum I'm facing in regard to what is public and what is private. A similar example she has come across often in her studies is with pregnant women or women of child bearing age. While the woman may be competitive within the scope of a job, it is not uncommon for an alternate candidate to be chosen simply to avoid the potential of dealing with maternity leave. There are many sides to this debate, but the bigger picture involves uncharted territory on privacy issues raised in the context of our modern society.

Walking through reasoning for my individual case she reminds me of the greater circumstances involved. There are many factors beyond my control, including coordinating the schedules of the two surgeons who will perform the operation, confirming insurance coverage, and Mom's availability to help take care of me during my initial recovery. Without a spouse or alternative means to support myself, I am solely responsible for securing and maintaining my financial stability. Finally, health matters are very personal and aside from the time off I will need to take for recovery, mine don't affect my ability to accomplish the job.

Putting it into perspective I acknowledge that full disclosure leaves room for my employers to weigh out the options based on what is best for the company, not me. I can't blame them for that. Similarly, it's my responsibility to take care of myself and exercise my right to privacy. I am feeling more comfortable with the situation and now all I have to worry about is their response which is out of my control anyway.

A week later I broach the subject with my employers and am pleasantly surprised. I tell my boss I was diagnosed in January, then the first scheduling fell through in May. Now, I have finally been approved to go through with it, but have a 90 day window in which the approval will be valid. I offer to work with the company calendar to find the best possible time to schedule. He reassures me that they will work with whatever time off I need to take. He also is understanding of the urgency of my time frame and encourages me to call in immediately to get a date on the books. I call in and am given one option: October 31st, 2011.

Mile marker

<u>Journal Entry - August 30th, 2011</u>
Here are some of the things I've been feeling stressed about or that are making me sad. I just turned 30 (generally a major mile marker where you assess where your life is at) and I am:

-single

-financially insecure

-getting more and more out of shape trying not to aggravate my hip

-not allowed to dance

-unsure of how recovery will go

-giving up the jobs I had, left me distanced from the people associated with them.

Art in the Dark

It's "Art in the Dark" time again. Every August, AWOL does a show where we hire a professional rigger to string cables between the trees out in the forest just outside of Portland. From the cables we hang our aerial equipment, then set up stages with full theatre lighting and present a completely original evening-length work under the stars. It's usually one of my favorite times of year. We rehearse the whole month of August in the park. I get to hang out with some of my best friends, laugh and play in the woods, and then finally perform a show that anyone who has ever seen would easily agree is an overall truly magical experience.

This year, with the uncertainty of when surgery would eventually be scheduled, as well as my doctor's recommendation to refrain from dancing, I am not in the show. Instead I sit on the periphery watching rehearsals.

A kinesthetic person already, I have also spent years honing my ability to learn choreography quickly, and whenever I watch dance, I experience it on a physical level as if it's being replicated it in my own body even as I sit still. As I watch, my body aches with the desire to hop on stage and join in. This is what my doctor warned me about. Physically nothing has changed about my condition so I could be participating if I felt like it, but I run the risk of damaging the joint further and have made the decision to avoid increasing those risks in addition to avoiding the pain. This whole week I think I've gone a bit numb trying to protect myself. I don't dare allow myself to experience extreme emotions, either happy or sad, in case they instigate a meltdown.

On closing night of the official show, as I was leaving the park, Eek (a former student, now youngest company member at age 16, who I fondly refer to as Eek though it's not her real name) came tearing through the forest to say goodbye to me, as I wouldn't be back to rehearsal until after my procedure. She gave me the biggest hug, and when I pulled away I saw tears in her eyes and she said, "I hope your hip gets better." The tone of her voice and the look on her face seemed sad and nervous like she was asking me to tell her it was going to be okay. While I was still struggling to convince myself, I felt compelled to be a role model. I cried all the way home, hoping I would be able to face surgery with enough strength to make my little Eek proud!

A warm and fuzzy heart

Earlier in the summer I was talking to one of my aerial students (Angela) and she was asking for an update on what was going on with my surgery. Since I had stopped teaching in May, no one in the classes really knew what had happened. I explained to her that I had technically been approved for surgery though at the time was still jobless leaving me stuck between two essential priorities. Clearly I wanted to move forward with restoring my physical health, but I also had my financial security, both present and future to consider. I was going in round-about circles telling her that I had no idea what to do and didn't even feel capable of making the decision of which to prioritize first. I had been told by Jean from Dr. Holt's office, that I would need to make a $3,000 deposit on the day of surgery, yet being jobless had swept up my meager savings account and I didn't know where that money was going to come from.

To call Angela pro-active would be an understatement. Upon hearing this news and witnessing my sense of defeat, she rapidly developed a plan to hold a benefit for me. Knowing that Vanessa, another aerial student, who also took my Pilates and yoga classes at Adidas, would be happy to assist, as well as be a valuable resource in planning the event, she recruited Vanessa's help and together they planned the event from start to finish.

October 8th, 2011

The benefit was last night and consisted of live music, performances by my advanced aerial students (including Angela and Vanessa,) more performances by AWOL, and a DJ. They put together a raffle which included 21 donated items ranging from Adidas gear to wine tastings to hula hooping lessons. A few of the more pricey contributions included a two-night stay at the Timberline Lodge on Mt. Hood, a full wellness package including acupuncture treatments, and an aerial performance for a private event were put in a silent auction. All the concessions were donated, including two kegs from Widmere Brewing Co., two cases of wine from a local bar (the owner of which recently discovered that his baby girl had hip dysplasia too), and catering, which served pulled pork sandwiches and lentil soup.

It was truly one of the most surreal things I have ever experienced. People I knew from every corner of my life came, as well as plenty of people I have never met! One story, that to me perfectly represents the warm and fuzzy essence of the evening: my friends Damien and Anastasia recently got engaged and were doing engagement photos the afternoon before the event. In casual conversation during the shoot their plans for the evening came up, and they told the photographer about the benefit and a little bit about my story. At the end of the photo shoot the photographer says, "Why don't you just take the check you were going to write me and write it to Emily." ...Speechless.

The entire evening I was flooded with support and well wishes from both friends and strangers. The audience not only loved the show, but seemed genuinely happy to be there, and everyone was impressed at the turnout. Nearly 200 people! Between ticket sales, concessions, and raffle, it brought in around $4,000, all going towards my surgery costs. In addition to that, we added a donate button to my website and I have been receiving contributions from both friends and friends of friends who couldn't make it to the show, but wanted to support me.

In the event itself and the stories surrounding it, I am completely stunned at the at the generosity and support of the community around me. During one of the most challenging moments of my life, and in the midst of the weakness I feel from losing my job, my health, and my identity all at once, a little angel popped down to remind me of all of the people who care. Even the ones that don't have to. And any time I felt overwhelmed by being completely on the receiving end of this, Vanessa kept reminding me that it's all a karmic cycle. She said I've touched many lives through teaching and convinced me that my students are honored to be able to give something back. She also reminded me that in the future, whether it's the people here for me now or not, someone will need to call upon me to be their strength and I will know exactly what to do.

It's time

<u>Journal Entry - 10:30 pm, Sunday, October 30th, 2011</u>
Surgery is tomorrow but I'm feeling quite calm about it at the moment. I am confident in my own ability to be strong and recover. The only thing left to be nervous about are complications. My surgeon has told me again and again that I am an ideal patient. I'm young and healthy so will heal quickly, I'm thin (which means they don't have to dig too far) and the surgery is nearly "textbook" because it isn't due to an accident or trauma.

I feel in such a better place to go through with this now than in May. I had many wonderful adventures this summer, a packed past month, and now we're approaching weather that makes you want to stay in anyway. Furthermore, I'm surrounded by the most wonderful people I can imagine. My list of cheerleaders just seems to keep growing. I feel very loved. I often feel down about not having a romantic love in my life, but what I'm experiencing now is so amazing. It's not just one person, but a whole community offering care and support. In romantic love you are often dependent on the other person's reactions, whims, and flaws. In this kind, it's everywhere you look and you can never be alone. I truly believe that this happiness in my heart will be the most powerful facilitator of my recovery.

Part Five

The big day

October 31st, 2011

4:30 am
   I wake up and take my second shower with the hot pink antibacterial soap provided for me at my pre-op appointment. I have not been allowed to eat or drink anything since last night, nor to even brush my teeth in case I accidentally swallow any water or toothpaste. Clean on the outside, empty on the inside.

5:30 am
   Mom and I arrive at the hospital. I was told to bring only the clothes on my back and my identification.

6:00-9:00 am
   I dress in my given gown and socks, and settle myself in the rolling hospital bed. I am asked to confirm my name, date of birth, procedure to be done, and location of procedure multiple times by various people. They draw an X on my left hip to indicate that is where surgery should occur. They take my vitals. My IV is placed. I wait patiently and cooperate as needed while preparation continues around me. Then Mom is asked to leave. At this exact moment I feel more nervous for her than I do for me. I will pass the time in an unconscious state completely unaware of anything until I come out. I imagine her hoping to fill the next nine hours with any distraction she can think of so as to avoid worrying and wondering how it is going. I suspect the hours will tick by slowly.

As they prepare to place the epidural (which will include a needle in my spine), I inhale some light laughing gas to desensitize me to the process. With the epidural in place, and the anesthesia beginning to kick in, I am ready for action.

9:00 am
Wheeled down the hall to the operating room, I am aware that I'm moving from one place to another though have no sense of the pathway we're taking. I see people around me, but their faces possess no detail. When we arrive they continue to ask me questions, and I believe I am answering them, though I have no idea where that capacity is coming from as my head seems to be floating off into space. A brief moment of distinct consciousness occurs as I am caught off guard by the doctors strapping my ankles and wrists to the table. A clear flash of images about what is about to take place speeds through my mind. I attempt to combat the fear by making a joke and say to the doctor, *Are these straps so I don't wake up half way through and kick you in the face?* Blackness.

1 hour
2 hours
3 hours
4 hours
5 hours
6 hours
7 hours

4:00 pm
I wake up in the recovery room. The only pain I'm experiencing is where my obliques have been stretched, the rest numbed by the epidural. I remain fairly vacant as I proceed to watch the clock tick tick tick.
5:00
6:00
7:00

Mom begs the nurses to let her in to the recovery room to sit with me.

8:00

9:30 pm

I begin to get impatient. My blood pressure is extremely low at 70/40 and they won't release me from the recovery room to go up to my hospital bed until it's consistently at 99/50. So we sit and wait, wait, wait. Neither Mom or I understand what factors are involved in helping get my blood pressure up to the allowable level before they let me go upstairs. I am so cold, yet covered in so many blankets I feel like I'm stuck under six feet of sand.

11:00 pm

Finally, an anesthesiologist arrives and decides to turn off my epidural for a few hours to see if that helps. When I was originally advised to get the epidural I was concerned about anything that could increase complications. I consulted Alexis who, in addition to being very medically knowledgeable, has gone through major back surgery. I was curious what she had learned from her personal experience, and if she thought the epidural would be a good idea. She did. She described the potential scene of emerging from anesthesia with the type of mind blowing pain inevitable for this type of procedure, completely disoriented and flooded with intense panic over how things went.

1:00 am

My epidural has been off for the past two hours, and I am finally admitted to my hospital room. I know nothing about how I get there. This is what Alexis had warned me of. The pain is searing and utterly debilitating. When we arrive in my hospital room, Mom immediately informs the nurse that while they turned off the epidural in the recovery room, no one has given me any meds, to which the nurse offers, "Well, what would she like?" Between the pain and exhaustion I am in pure survival mode, my consciousness verging on shut-down to escape the ferocity of my body's current state. I indignantly reply (possibly in a low shout), "What, do you have a *menu*? Shouldn't the doctor have sent instructions??" Startled into action, the nurse gives me a shot of morphine to take the edge off, then fills me with Oxycodone. Gradually the pain becomes dulled just enough that I am able to drift to sleep. After a long day, Mom goes home to get some rest as well.[1]

---

[1] See Additional Resources section at the end of the book for a diagram of the surgery performed.

The other side

Tuesday, November 1st

5:30 am
    I am rudely awakened when the lights to my hospital room flick on and before I've even opened my eyes my arm has been cinched by a rubber band and a gruff looking nurse hovers above with a needle. My head swimming in a state of drug induced, sleep deprived grogginess, I demand to know what she thinks she's doing?! She informs me that she's taking blood. (Each time they had to draw blood leading up to surgery it was not pretty. The prick didn't bother me, the needle would go in, but about 30 seconds in it would all take a turn for the worse. My blood pressure would drop dramatically, my head would become light, and the room would turn into a box of hot pink bubbles, then fade to black.) At this moment, my extreme aversion for this experience sprang into action despite my current foggy state, and I tore my arm away, declaring, "I had surgery less than 24 hours ago and do not have enough blood to give you!" Both surprised and irritated by my defiance, she huffs away, promising she is required to get it sooner or later.

8:15 am
    They still don't have my pain under control when two physical therapists arrive. One is a young woman with a very stern demeanor, the other is a middle aged man who has a bit of a hippie-like ease about him. It is clear that they aren't the most compatible team. The man begins wading slowly into the plan for today when the woman abruptly interrupts requesting I sit up and get going. Half way through my attempt at sitting up I look at her helplessly yet she refuses to offer assistance. Pain aside, my obliques had been stretched out of the way in metal retractors for seven hours during the procedure and don't seem to be communicating with my brain or able to

function. I grip the side rails of my bed, making the IV affixed to the top of my hand stab in. After multiple different attempts to maneuver myself up, and finally with a little assistance, I am able to sit up and bring my legs over the edge of the bed, but immediately shock waves of pain go searing through my body. I scream. The kind that seems to involuntarily erupt from the body. All reason and control are out the window with mind numbing pain and I am crying and writhing. Multiple nurses run in. One shoots a double dose of morphine through my IV as the others manage to lay me back down. I'm light-headed and shaking with a deep nauseated feeling creeping up. My body has gone into shock mode and I can't settle down or relax. I can hardly breathe enough to speak and everyone in the room has a look of panic. The physical therapists decide that's probably all for the day and leave in a rush.

  The day nurse writes on the giant white board the goal for the day: PAIN CONTROL.

fog
meds
sleep
peace

  Yes, despite the physical pain, there is an unexpected and partially unidentifiable change in my mental state that feels somehow peaceful. A friend who came to visit the following day admitted that she expected me to be miserable, in pain, full of drugs, and cranky about being stuck in a hospital bed all day. Yet, ever since I woke up in recovery and Dr. Holt came in to check on me, and told me all went well, *no complications,* I've been washed over with a strange lightness. I've been climbing and clamoring towards this moment. I've navigated through so much darkness to get here and danced a delicate march towards whatever outcome was on the other side. The other side! So many possibilities muddied my vision of what the other side was going to look like but here I am! I've hardly arrived. I'm barely past the tipping point. This isn't over, there's still so much ahead, so much uncertainty left and yet a crucial component that lay outside of my influence is complete, *no complications*. The pain is unearthly, but I've lived with pain. Pain has been a part of me. *This* is extreme, but *this* is temporary, and *this* is the beginning of the other side.

30 year old granny

I've been sliding in and out of varying states of consciousness. Day and night I have to take meds every three hours. My alert energy sourcing from the cleared mind-space of being on the other side is contrasted with the fogginess that rolls in with the meds. On the one hand, I've greeted visitors and joked with nurses in the appropriate hospital humor relating to backless gowns and being a 30 year old granny with a walker. On the other, one day I fell asleep while brushing my teeth, waking up who knows how much later, with toothbrush in hand and no one around.

Unfortunately, my favorite granny perk is about to come to an end. They put a catheter in while I was under anesthesia, and for the last day or so I haven't had to think about peeing. It just goes away when it needs to and someone empties a bag of barely yellow fluid near my bed every so often. I've been hydrating like a maniac, and why not, with such a slick convenient system! Now they want to take it out, which I'm opposed to, but follow their medical advice this time around.

Mere hours later I regret it entirely. For one, a full bladder against a broken pelvis is less than comfortable. But also, this means a five step, walker-assisted hobble to the bathroom and I must admit I'm a bit nervous every time I get out of bed. I'm not allowed to put weight on my left leg for the next six weeks, though I think I can work with that. My concern is somewhere else... I mean, they sawed my pelvis in half, then of course screwed it back together, but who's to say when I stand up it isn't just going to fall apart? OK, unrealistic I know, but the mental picture has already been created.

Time to begin the process of my first post surgery toilet excursion. I can't use any of the muscles surrounding the hip joint so as not to pull the bones out of their new alignment, so I have to have Mom lift my leg out of bed while I attempt to handle the other three quarters of my body. Sat up, now I must rest. A few friends have just arrived and I let them know what a momentous occasion they've happened upon and talk them through my mental preparation for the next step. I gingerly make my way to the standing position, when again, I need assistance from Mom to lift my left foot and reposition it behind me since I'm not allowed to use the muscles to keep it lifted in front. Forward progression requires what I consider to be more of a 'hop-ble.' When you have access to weight-bearing on both legs you can hobble along behind the walker. Since I only am allowed to use one leg, I have to take a little hop with each step hence, the hop-ble. One step on my good leg, then I press all my weight off the other leg, swing it forward, then lower myself back down. It's like doing repetitive press-ups on a set of parallel bars...while I'm not weak on a normal day, circumstantially this is exhausting! Once in the bathroom I clench the handicap rail and lower myself down to sitting. It's tough to understand, but in the medical field the pelvis is separated into three front to back columns. The bones you sit on are part of a different column than the hip socket itself, which is why I can sit down but not stand.

    I reverse the whole process to get back in bed. All in all, this first pee was a 20-30 minute start-to-finish endeavor. I'm spent and already dreading the next elimination.

Bring me a steak

It's Day Three in the hospital now. I am starting to get used to the routine. Since this is a teaching hospital there are so many people attending to me at various times of day that I sometimes get confused as to who is who, or who I should ask if I need something. Today a medically dressed person, who I have never seen before, came in and declared he was prepping me for a blood transfusion.

Sure, I'm totally weak, white as a ghost, and they have said my blood count is low, but I only thought a transfusion was a potential during the procedure. I also very much dislike the thought someone else's blood being pumped into my veins. Finding this news both unexpected and unsettling, I inquire further.

"Well," says unknown doctorish type, "your blood count is low, and due to your other symptoms you may be a bit anemic."

Right, and mild anemia in these temporary circumstances is dangerous to me how? Don't my charts indicate that I walked a full 20 steps down the hall yesterday? I'm practically an Olympian on my walker! I'm able to speak, to pee, and to eat, which concludes all of the obligations I have at current. Once again...."I'm not sure if I fully understand the necessity."

He reassures me with, "If you were 70 it wouldn't even be a question."

Hmmm, last time I checked I'm not, nor do I look, like a 70 year old. Clearly the "why" question isn't getting me anywhere. Though once again, I'm washing in and out of consciousness and I don't feel I have the capacity in my drug induced state to be discussing such decisions. The doctor leaves without further comment and the upcoming transfusion remains uncertain. Later in the day Dr. Holt arrives to clear up the matter.

We revisit the topic of why, and this time I add to my questions "So, are there any other options?"

"You could try to eat a steak."

"Then bring me a steak!"

Steak successful. No transfusion. Color back in the cheeks. Blood count up. I much preferred the simple solution.

Hospital discharge

It's my last day in the hospital and I'll admit I am starting to get impatient. The docs have agreed to let me go home, but I have to have one final physical therapy appointment before I am officially approved for discharge. This appointment is quite helpful as it is here they teach me things like how to get in the car and go up stairs minding my restrictions. The physical therapist hands me my crutches and two steps in I'm already failing. I learn that the best way to use crutches is to wedge the top of the crutch into my ribs a few inches below my armpit. Brilliant!! While still mildly uncomfortable, this positioning prevents dumping all my weight onto my tender armpits, though does require quite a bit more strength.

When we get to the physical therapy room, the therapist shows me how to navigate the stairs by putting both crutches in one hand as one support while using the railing on the other side to be my other support. I go up the stairs fine. On the way down the therapist spots me by holding onto my velcro close gown. Luckily, Mom is there and can see the multifaceted disaster if I were to fall and she spots my actual body on the other side.

In addition to other set-like items, the room possesses a pretend car. I am shown how to align my body to sit down in the seat, swivel slightly to lift my good leg in the car, then use my hands to get my second leg in. I pass all my requirements and the therapist is very impressed with how quickly I master each.

Now all that's standing in the way of freedom from this place is getting my prescription filled, gathering my belongings, and getting a wheelchair to take me to the curb. I'm resting in bed after my therapy, but would rather be resting at home. Mom goes to fill my prescription on the other side of the hospital. I pressed the button to have a nurse come check on me, but it's been awhile. I need my ice replaced and help packing up my room. No one seems to be responding to my nurse button, so I get up and do it myself. When Mom returns she's astonished to see me standing on one leg near my neat piles of stuff ready to go.

They wheel me out to the curb and I triumphantly conclude the hospital portion of my recovery!

Withdrawal

November 6th, 2011

    My first full day "home" which for the next few weeks is Aunt Becky's house, I woke up feeling pretty miserable, actually. Mornings are always worse and then afternoons feel better. Last night, Aunt Lulu and Uncle Jim joined my in-home recovery unit for the weekend as they happened to be passing through town. Lulu is a nurse so it's great timing as we're trying to figure out how to organize my routine.
    I am set up on a day bed in the corner of a living area that is a big open space with the kitchen and dining room. I have a half bathroom of my own just through the laundry room near the garage, all on ground level. Fortunately, that allows me to be stair free for most of my daily needs. The one challenge we've been aware of, but haven't addressed, is that the shower is up two sets of stairs. With the extra help from Lu and Jim I decided it would be excellent timing to take my first shower in six days.
    The hospital staircase I practiced on had only four stairs, so two flights seems daunting. After talking through a plan, Becky and Jim decide it may just be easiest to carry me. With one arm over Becky's shoulder, and the other over Jim's, I lift my legs from underneath me and they make it up the first set of stairs. The second set is narrower and the three of us side-by-side hardly fit, but we finally reach the top. I have purchased a shower chair that allows me to sit instead of stand precariously on one leg in the slippery tub. Once in the bathroom, Mom has to help me get undressed. Then I sit holding onto the chair to stabilize while she lifts my leg over the edge of the tub. Finally, I'm in and luckily there is a detachable shower head so Mom keeps the water on me while I soap up.
    I can't help but feel a bit like both a small child and a plant. A small child, because when I accidentally drop the soap, Mom has to pick it up for me since I can't bend far

enough to reach. A plant, because Mom looks like she's watering the garden standing above me with the detachable shower hose. I laugh about it to ease the awkwardness, but Mom doesn't seem to be fazed. I suppose that's a motherhood thing that perhaps one day I'll understand.

After reversing the process to get out of the tub and dressed, Becky and Jim return to carry me back down. The way down poses a bigger problem than the way up. Since I'm not allowed to bring my hip into flexion, my only option is to bend my knee and keep the foot up. Unfortunately, it doesn't bend quite far enough to avoid my foot bumping down the stairs behind me so Mom has to trail behind holding my foot off the ground so it doesn't get jarred. No harm done, just precarious and a little painful but I make it back to bed in one piece.

After assessing my med schedule, there's some debate on whether I need quite the dosage I was on in the hospital. It does seem excessive, though hard to tell whether that's necessary or not. I'm also going on Day Six of no bowel movement, likely caused by being on so many meds. In the end, reducing my meds becomes the new goal.

I took my last Oxycodone at 7:15 am. I took only one in comparison to the two to three they would give me in the hospital. Then there was the whole shower adventure which distracted me for some time. After that Alexis, my acupuncturist, came to visit and to give me a treatment. She put needles in my abdomen to help with my digestive concerns. My hip was also extremely swollen still, so she mixed up a concoction of chinese herbs to rub on the skin around my scar while the needles were in. After an hour like this, the swelling had miraculously and dramatically reduced! No such immediate progress with the digestion, but hopefully it will take it's course.

By the time Alexis leaves, I feel exhausted by the constant stimulation of the day. I get up to go to the bathroom. Sitting on the toilet, hoping for some movement to occur post acupuncture, I start feeling extremely weak. I call for some assistance and when Mom comes to help me she realizes that I won't make it back to bed on my own. Jim and Becky are summoned once again to carry me back. I am not just weak, my body is now ice cold and I'm shivering to the point of convulsions, yet pouring sweat. The pain feels like it's splitting me in half, worsened by the fact that all my muscles have tensed with chill. Once I've been successfully tucked into bed, Mom and Lulu bring a hot pack to wrap around my stomach and then rub my legs until I can calm down a little. Still shaking uncontrollably, a deep nausea has set in. The discomfort is overwhelming and my breath is shallow.

    Lying helplessly in bed I drift in and out of consciousness through pain, nausea and discomfort while Mom and Lulu make three calls to the on-call doctor and two trips to the pharmacy. It's 5:30 pm and I finally take more Oxy. As it slowly takes effect, I am able to slip into a deep sleep and escape the suffering.

Setting the routine

While it's nice to be out of the hospital, we have had to work to set up the routine at home. Mom has a small notebook dedicated to my meds schedule. In addition to pain meds, I'm on about five other things just to keep my body functioning. Each pill has a different schedule and it can get very confusing. Some I need to take every few hours, some twice a day morning and night, one every day at exactly noon...etc., so Mom has decided to write it down each time I take something to be sure we keep track. A typical day looks about like this:

12:00 am	1 oxy (for pain)
2:00 am	1 oxy, 1 tylenol
4:30 am	3 oxy, 1 tylenol, 1 gabapentin (specifically for nerve pain)
8:30 am	2 senna (stool softener/laxative)
10:00 am	1 oxy, 1 tylenol, 1 zolfran (helps with nausea caused by excessive meds)
12:00 pm	rivaroxaban (prevents blood clotting)
1:00 pm	1 oxy, 1 tylenol
2:14 pm	1 oxy, 1 gabapentin
6:15 pm	1 oxy, 1 tylenol, 1 senna
10:00 pm	2 oxy, 1 zolfran, 1 gabapentin

One of the fears I had leading up to surgery is that I would go both mentally and physically insane during recovery while not being able to move and exercise regularly. I genuinely couldn't understand it. When you break your leg, you have a cast that prevents you from moving it. With a broken pelvis, clearly a cast option isn't available nor reasonable, but did they really trust *me* to just sit still on my own accord?? When I had asked the doctors to paint me a picture of how not to move and they looked at me as if they were being asked to explain the obvious. *Well, you don't move...* but it wasn't obvious to me! During the day I supposed I could focus on it more and constantly remind my body not to follow it's impulses, but at night how would I prevent my body from not wiggling all around like it usually does?

My surprising discovery both in the hospital and currently is that my brain is now utterly focused on a different objective. In this first two weeks my body has been working so hard to heal that my energy level is extraordinarily low and the impulses to move are subdued. I am also so exhausted from just walking across the room to go to the bathroom or sitting at the table to eat, that I need a three hour nap following such an expedition. Completely subconsciously, my brain has resigned itself to my fate of excessive rest and my body is following.

Another reason my brain is now in a different mode likely has to do with pain. Moving, quite frankly, hurts so much that it isn't very appealing anyway. All my muscles are stiff from so little movement, and the ones that were stretched or manipulated during surgery are weak and seem to be lacking neuromuscular connection. Going from lying to sitting is awkward because I have to simultaneously maneuver my leg with a leash which hooks around my foot, acting as my own puppet master. I've had to practice rolling over onto my stomach which requires gripping the steel railing of my day bed with one hand, and using my other hand to roll my pelvis over. I am also required to do exercises to keep the mobility in my hip joint, better described as having exercises done to me. I am not allowed to use my own muscles to do the exercises, so three times a day, someone else has to pick my leg up and move it around in circular motions while I just lay there.

    I will admit that being as medicated as I am is probably contributing to my ability to sit still as well. Mentally and physically I am much more indifferent than usual and am able to just let the time pass without concern of being productive. My primary objective is to rest and heal.

Epic poop

11:00 pm, November 7th, 2011

I feel awful. My stomach feels like someone pumped a balloon up inside it that is now taking up all the space and preventing my organs from functioning. It's November, yet I'm wearing a small night dress, my body too warm from medication to add any layers. I have to go to the bathroom so I grab my leg leash, gently hoist my leg out of bed, and walker my way to the toilet.

I sit down with great effort, desperately uncomfortable. I feel like I can't breathe. I've been hoping to poop for awhile. I feel like I have to poop now, but since my insides have turned to stone nothing ever happens. As I sit waiting, I grow even more uncomfortable. Maybe it is going to happen this time... maybe my body is finally ready! It's been six days. I start feeling nervous that no one is awake and my phone is back by the bed. Ugh, why did I leave it there?? I debate about what to do. Should I get back up and go retrieve my phone? What if halfway there I have an "emergency"? I'm not particularly speedy on my walker. Is this really happening? My nervousness about how helpless I am if things take a turn for the worse wins, and I walker back to the bed to grab my phone, then head back to the toilet. I call Mom who is upstairs sleeping.

"Mom, I'm on the toilet, I need you to come down."

When she arrives, I'm officially writhing in pain. Not only is a toilet seat disagreeable to a broken pelvis, but I also now have a rock solid boulder that feels halfway in, halfway out. I describe how it feels to Mom. It's one of those moments where the intensity of the scenario leaves no room for dignity.

I've been pushing, twisting my torso back and forth, massaging my abdomen, nothing is helping. I'm starting to sweat, the eerie feverish kind when it feels like all the blood runs from your body and you start to get light headed.

I'm writhing, I'm begging her to do something. She can't hold back a laugh and says, "What to do you want *me* to do??" I'm aware of the absurdity of my request and manage a small chuckle, but the situation is dire, I don't care who does what, this needs to be over with! She brings me a glass of orange juice.

After around 30 minutes of agony on the toilet, the boulder finally bursts through and my bowels empty. I'm shaking, sweating, freezing at this point and hardly strong enough to make it back to bed, my energy shot. Before I flush, I look at the culprit, which I am horrified to discover is about three inches in diameter. Mom says, "Well, that's just about what child birth feels like."

First outings

Journal Entry - November 9th, 2011
Feeling quite restless. The end.

    When I begin to reduce my meds and come back to my more usual mental state I feel progressively more stir crazy. I make Mom take me on a drive around Lake Oswego just so I can leave the house. Mom always makes fun of me when I paw at the window watching joggers go by. My lungs ache with the desire to be challenged. My heart longs to pump wildly, produce an invigorating sweat, charge my cells. The only thing that helps is knowing I am on the other side.

    A few days ago my friend Jessica, who also worked at Adidas, picked me up and took me to a big sample sale. The sample sales at Adidas happen about once a year and are complete chaos. You must have a badge to get in, then there are racks and racks of sample items priced between $3-$20 - the proceeds of which all go to charity. There is always a DJ, a keg, snacks, and everyone is jammed in a small room with clothing and shoes frantically flying off the racks.

    When we originally decided I would try to go, it sounded so wonderful to be able to see my former students and be in a social environment. I hadn't been out in three weeks! It happened to be a rainy night and I decided to use my walker again since crutches would be hard to set aside. We had to park two blocks away. Jess slowly walked alongside me as I tried to keep up a reasonable pace. One of my students saw me crossing the street and ran out to walk with us. He was surprised to see me and made many inquiries on our way to the door. Once inside, I was met with a number of different reactions. Some exclaimed, "You are INCREDIBLE! I can't believe you are out of bed already!" While some very honestly declared, "It's too strange to see you like this," and quickly looked away. Overall, the initial reaction of everyone that knew me was more like they saw an unexpected ghost.

While I enjoyed my time out, I didn't leave the house for three days following my little adventure, completely drained.

Journal Entry - November 17th, 2011
Wow, big day, I think I need a twelve hour nap...luckily I have time for that.

Finally, I'm ready to venture out again so Mom, Becky and I go out for sushi just down the street. We are seated in a booth, though unfortunately it is made of wood and has no padding so my tolerance for sitting here is low. After a short dinner I am getting quite uncomfortable and am ready to go. There is a large circular table next to us with a family at it. As I start getting my coat on and crutches ready, a little boy at the table, jumps out of his seat and runs around the corner (I assume to go the bathroom). I only notice because they had just received their food and I wonder why he waited until then. As I crutch my way around the corner I get struck with an immediate draft of cold air. I look forward to discover that the little boy had seen me gathering my crutches and leapt up to go hold the door for me! My heart feels instantly warm, such a small gesture, such a strong impact.

Bittersweet transition

Thanksgiving weekend and Mom and I pack up my shower chair, walker, crutches, and suitcases of clothes into my Mini Cooper and drive down to Eugene to be with family. On Thanksgiving day I start getting that chilled prickly feeling all over and hope I am not experiencing withdrawal symptoms again. I have just switched from Oxy to Vicoden and am not sure what the transition will be like. The day after Thanksgiving I wake up with a detrimental cold and spend the rest of the weekend miserable.

Getting sick was not part of the plan. Moving back to my own house Monday morning is the plan, and despite my sickness, I am determined to follow through. I am ready to at least pretend to be a real person again. I am also scheduled to return to work next week and am eager to start living a semi-normal schedule.

With prep for the transition underway, it feels more bittersweet than I expected. Mom left her own life for an entire month, planning to be with me for as long as I needed. Her sister Becky opened her home for us to stay for the unknown period of time. Now we're packing up my things and I'm leaving. I wasn't really expecting to experience nostalgia during this stage, but it seems to be creeping in.

Mom and I have spent a month hanging out, talking, cooking, and giggling a lot. I've always brought out the silly side in her, and perhaps she's where I got my silly side from. Part of the experience this past month has been the friendship that you develop with your parents when they cease to be the authoritative figures in your life and you are able to meet on a different level.

I remember back in my first year in college when my dad sent me a card. It said that he and Mom were now proud spectators of my life and trusted in my ability to shape it well. They were also now there to support my decisions and were excited to watch things unfold. I, of course cried when I read it, but also felt empowered to take responsibility for my future and make them proud. Throughout this whole surgery process Mom and Dad have done much more than spectate, but they have held true to being crucial supporters and it's something I never want to take for granted.

While strengthening the friendship and bond that Mom and I have as people, this has also given me a unique opportunity to be conscious of the parent/child bond on sort of a distant, past level. A glimpse at a time earlier in life when Mom and Dad put me in the tub, helped me go potty, got up multiple times a night to feed me. This time around, I was on a cognitive level to appreciate it and truly acknowledge the unconditional love and selflessness that goes with it.

There's no use hanging in this nostalgic place, but I can't help but feel simultaneously grateful that I have them, sad at Mom's leaving, yet excited to be returning to my life, and maybe curious as to if I will ever get to experience this type of bond with a child of my own.

A day in the life

Journal Entry - December 5th, 2011
No more bone pain. Not feeling overly exhausted. Incision healing well. Able to be completely, though perhaps creatively, independent. Starting week five post surgery, all that remains is frustration, discomfort and inconvenience.

Sleeping and cooking are two of my main enemies. Due to the minimal circulation, both in the left leg and really my whole body due to lack of good exercise, I don't produce my own body heat and it's tough to stay warm. I fill a water bottle with hot water to put at the foot of my bed at night, hoping that I'll be able to warm up the sheets a bit when I get in. Inevitably, I still feel chilled though, and bury myself in blankets since I can't curl my legs up under me. After three to four hours I usually wake up again and am awake for an hour or two battling the discomfort of only being able to lie flat on my back or flat on my front, but not in between.

Waking up in the morning isn't much better because the first thing I have to do is make breakfast. In our kitchen everything is between two and five steps away. With only one leg and any mode of transportation (walker or crutches) tying up both hands, it's an overly daunting task getting the oatmeal from the cupboard, then the water in the pan, then the orange juice from the fridge. Then once breakfast is made, I can't carry it out to the table anyway so I eat standing on one leg or sitting on the folding chair my housemates brought into the kitchen for me.

Perhaps the most unsettling thing is that while I'm back at my house, I'm not even in my own room. My bedroom is upstairs, which I can't get to due to steep, narrow stairs with no railing. One of my housemates agreed to switch our beds so I could sleep downstairs. While that's been an absolute necessity, it is frustrating to not be in my own room, with access to and places to put my stuff, and the general feeling of personal space. It all seems so petty and *small compared to what I've gone through so far, but since I'm feeling so much better in every other way it magnifies the irritation of my limitations.*

My final gripe: All I can wear is sweat pants and slippers unless someone helps me get dressed, so I feel frumpy all the time.

Moment of truth

December 7th, 2011

    Tomorrow is the moment of truth and I'm terrified. My six week appointment has to be scheduled on a Thursday since that's the day Dr. Holt is in clinic, which leaves me the choice of scheduling technically at five and a half weeks or six and a half weeks post surgery. Originally, I had it scheduled for the six and a half week mark, but I am getting impatient and really think I might be ready earlier. I can't imagine that four days makes that big of a difference, but what do I know.

    On the one hand, I'm terrified that he will say I came in too early and send me away for even longer than if I had waited. On the other, I rested, ate well, mostly cut out coffee, alcohol, and sugar for six weeks, and feel like I've taken the best possible care of my body that one could. Not to mention, what Dr. Holt had pointed out in the beginning which is that I'm young, healthy, and would heal quickly. I take my chances and move my appointment up to the Thursday before.

    I always schedule my appointments at 8:20 am or simply, first thing in the morning so he doesn't have the chance to get backed up. This time I wasn't able to get in until 11:40 am. Sitting in the familiar waiting room, with many elderly people around me, I wait. Hardly able to contain myself, I nervously play with my phone, text people, search for distractions that keep me in the moment. I can't read, my focus will just drift away from the page and back to the anticipation of my name getting called. With the tension building in my body for two hours, I finally get called back.

    Dr. Holt has a gorgeous office with a picture window view of Mt. Hood. It's a bright sunny day, and as I walk by I look in at the stunning view. I also catch a glimpse of him reviewing my x-rays that had been taken just moments ago. My stomach is in my throat, or some other muddled arrangement of my insides from what should be their proper location! My eyes are wide and alert and I'm ready to take in every word he says.

When he enters the room he asks how I am. I want to shout, *Get to the point, am I allowed to walk or not!*, but instead I engage in some conversation about how my recovery is going. Finally, he gives me the news that I am cleared to start weight bearing! I jump up (figuratively) to test it out. Now it's Dr. Holt who looks petrified. Sometimes I feel like a cartoon character in his office as he often looks alarmed at my level of animation. I gently ease my crutches from under my armpits and attempt to stand on my left leg. The sensation is unlike anything I've ever felt. My leg doesn't feel like my own. Shrunk to half of it's original size, it doesn't look like mine either.

He waits for my response. I report back that it feels just like a noodle and that I can't possibly put my full weight on it as it certainly wouldn't know how to hold me up. He advises that I will probably need to use a crutch or a cane on that side for about a month before the strength returns. I am nothing less than elated and realize that I paid very little attention to any of the details of what he said. I can walk!!

By the time I leave, it's around 2:00 pm and I eagerly call Mom to let her know the news. My voice is jumping up and down as I describe how it felt.

Two days later, I started feeling like the one crutch is causing more problems than it is solving. I have to twist my back and hunch to one side with every other step and I feel all out of alignment. I have been practicing standing still on two legs endlessly and decide the strength will only build if I use it. I invite my friend Spring over and she takes a short video of the momentous occasion of my very first unsupported steps. As I proudly put the crutch off to the side I take five small, limpy steps towards the camera, Spring mockingly narrating, "Baby's first steps! Can you sing that one Christmas carol you know?"

Part Six

The unexpected visitor

Rewind. There's a part of this story I've left out.

When I wake up in the recovery room there's a text waiting for me that says *You have been in my thoughts all morning*. It's from Kalen and my heart jumps a little. He sent me encouraging words last night before I went to bed and now this?

A few days later he arrives in my hospital room one evening after work. Vanessa is visiting that night also. I take a little cruise down the hall, of about 20 arduous steps using the energy of my visitors being there to keep my motivation up. They walk along beside me at a snail's pace. Their faces are a mixture of concern, surprise, and encouragement as they watch this highly effortful process unfold.

After my walk I get back in bed and my energy begins to dwindle. Vanessa decides to head home, but Kalen stays a little longer. The strangest part is this is the first time we've ever been one-on-one. We have hung out in group settings before, but now here we are in the most awkward of circumstances for just the two of us. My face is still swollen with all the fluids they've been pumping into me, and my skin isn't quite the right tone yet as my blood count is still low. I disregard my temptation to imagine his perception of me from the outside and decide that being self-conscious has no place in the hospital. Before he goes he asks if I need anything, then comes over and reaches for my hand. While holding my hand between his he says, "You look good," and then after a long pause leaves me to rest.

I don't even recognize the sensation I'm having. There have been a few guys who tempted my desire for a companion in the midst of all this chaos. I felt weak and scared and alone and desperately wanted someone to prop me up when I couldn't do it myself. I met one guy within days of my first appointment with Dr. Holt. There was no way around letting him in on the crazy transition I was about to live out. Instead of going off running and screaming, he proved to be very understanding. He let me cry, he acknowledged my right to be sad, he would cook me dinner after a long day. I felt so comfortable around him and so grateful for his presence, and yet something told me our connection felt ultimately more like a friendship and I couldn't avoid glimpsing into the future after it all and seeing us move in separate ways. After a few months, I decided that it would be very selfish of me to keep him around if I couldn't imagine a future for us.

Another guy seemed to leap on the idea of being a knight in shining armor. He spoiled me and gave me massages and tried to prove what a brilliant man-of-my-life he could be. I felt uneasy and misrepresented. He wanted to be with someone who truly was weak and needed him, but deep in my heart I knew this was a temporary place for me and didn't represent who I am.

A third eligible bachelor originally came off as understanding but ultimately took my least favorite approach of trying to fix things for me (i.e., offering to look over my resume, then telling me how to go about getting a job.) But he was unhappy in his own job and with his own life, and I had a suspicion that focusing on the repair of mine was somehow making him feel better. He didn't last long.

The delightful thought of having an intimate partner to help me through this had long since dissipated. I fully planned to go through it alone.

Kalen was first introduced to me through Vanessa, who initially tried to set us up. After months of hearing about him, we finally met, but he was dating someone so we just became acquaintance type friends. That was about a year ago. We actually discovered we had more than one mutual friend and so crossed paths at parties or floating the river. I also ran into him many other times at various street fairs, events, or just walking along the sidewalk. In the month before surgery I seemed to see more of him than ever.

While my surgery was on the official date of Halloween (a Monday), I tried to distract myself the weekend before by socializing and going to costume parties. He kept popping up at all the same parties I was at, though not coincidentally, having asked for my number the week before and inquiring as to where I'd be. Despite the sense I got that he was intentionally trying to be near me, he seemed to have a simultaneous elusive quality.

It seemed obvious to me that his timing couldn't have been worse. I would be living at my aunt's house just out of town for the next month and I imagined that in the next two months of being unable to walk I'd be fairly detached from any type of social world. I'm not sure if he really knew the extent of my circumstance, but I followed my usual policy of holding up my end of the communication and finally told him he was sending me mixed messages.

He called the next day (the day before surgery) to say, "I like you and I'm attracted to you and I'm not trying to send you mixed messages."

Oh well, I thought, *irrelevant now, see you in two months maybe.*

Always there

Released from the hospital, I'm back at my aunt's house now and he's here, again. Every week, *twice* a week, he's comes to visit me. He sits on the love seat right next to me, always checking in, to make sure his sitting there isn't bothering my hip. It's funny though, because there is plenty of other furniture in the room. When my other friends come to visit they sit on the big squishy chair adjacent to the love seat, which I always claim because it's my most comfortable spot. That's how I know something feels different. That and other things.

He usually comes straight from work around five and then stays until midnight. I'm currently residing at my aunt Becky's house so he has dinner with me, Mom, and Becky. I have my own little living room and nook where a bed is set up for me just off the kitchen and dining room. After dinner, Mom and Becky move in to the main living room and Kalen and I end up back on the love seat in front of the fireplace. The first few nights we talk until the wee hours. One night we tried to watch a movie, but then decided we preferred just getting to know each other. Every day we have an endless stream of text messages back and forth. He checks in on how I'm doing.

Text conversation - November 9th, 2011

Excruciating pain at the moment, not sure why. Maybe it has to do with going 5 hours without pain meds when I usually take them every 3.

So sorry to hear that, I can't imagine.

Text conversation - November 11th, 2011

> *What's the latest news on the healing?*

Minor melt down today. Just sick of either being in pain or uncomfortable. Went to bed early now up doing exercises so I can sleep. Trying to regain patience.

> *Ahhh sorry :(Can I visit you this weekend? Hang in there, you really can do it.*

I know, this is kinda the first bump but won't be the last. I'll get there. Think of how enthusiastic I'll be for physical therapy!

Or we continue conversations from the night before, like when he made fun of me for being ridiculously layered up and huddled under a blanket, while he doesn't even wear a coat outside despite it being November.

Text conversation - November 14th, 2011

For example, down to a t-shirt at work, still too hot. Everyone else is wearing jackets.

> *For example, I wore socks with my slippers today and still have cold feet. Should have made you lay in my bed before you left last night, was cold for 30 min before sleep took over.*

That sucks! But I was so tired I would have fallen asleep instantly and you wouldn't have been able to move me.

        True, and I can't even carry a plate across the room so that could've proved difficult.

You could have leveraged me out with a crutch maybe.

        I probably would have just kept you.

And always, I let him know how much it means to me.

<u>Text conversation - November 6th, 2011</u>

Thanks for coming to visit, I enjoy your company.

        Visiting you ain't no obligation, I look forward to it. But I'm glad you like my company. I like talking with you quite a lot. Peculiar circumstance, but good as any.

The fact that you're willing to join me within the circumstance is all the better.

<u>Text conversation - November 14th, 2011</u>

        Hope you're getting some rest. Sending healing thoughts your way regularly.

I know you are. And whether I've sufficiently expressed it or not, it really means a lot to me how kind you've been and how often you check in on me.

Well, I like you.

Well good. I will still give you credit for being wonderful because I like you too.

<u>Text conversation - November 22nd, 2011</u>

My favorite nights are the night you visit. It's definitely contributing to my healing. :)

I have healing powers! I really like talking to you. Same wavelength it seems. Have a wonderful holiday. See you next week!

My heart feels like it's floating.

I wonder why I'm letting him get this close when I refused to let others take care of me like this. But I also feel confused, and desperately want to ask him why he's here or what it means. I don't, for fear that he will begin to question it himself and change his mind. The last thing I want to do is lose the support, the distraction, and the smile I get from our interactions.

I don't quite know how to handle this within the context of my lost identity. Usually, when I meet a fella who might be of interest, I have many things going on. I have multiple jobs to talk about, a lively social life, I can tell them about my dancing. Eventually, maybe I'll invite him to my next show where he will catch a glimpse of my passion. When I am performing, I feel confident and alive. He'll see my physical strength and capabilities and finally begin to understand the necessity of all the hours and evenings spent at rehearsal. But here I am, using a walker to maneuver myself around, unable to lift my own leg into bed, my once toned body now just flesh hanging off the bone.

Then there are the insecurities I have facing my career. I am on the mend but it is still unclear the extent to which I'll be able to return to doing what I love. While I usually have a path, or at the very least a string of idealistic concepts for my future I currently feel unable to entertain those for fear of them not being available to me. Instead I feel strangely hollow.

He assures me that my lost sense of identity is an illusion. He says he's impressed with how I've handled myself through this process and can see my passion and drive.

Digging deeper

The first night he came over was shortly after I got out of the hospital. He stayed so late everyone else went to bed and I had to ask him to help me lift my leg into bed and then let himself out.

Sometimes he would take me on a drive just so I could get out of the house. One day he took me to a park. It was rainy November, the ground was a little slippery and I was only 13 days past surgery. He walked extremely close to me, attentive to my every movement, ready to catch me if I faltered, checking in with my energy level regularly. We took a little break on a bench as I wanted to stay outside as long as possible. My hands were cold from holding on to my crutches and he rubbed them between his to warm them. It was his favorite park from childhood and held many sentimental memories. Still in the initial stages of getting to know him, this was an unusual occurrence when he offered up personal information about himself.

There have been other times when we talked about him, but more often than not he keeps the focus on me. He has a bit of a nervous twitch that I don't understand. Sometimes I wonder if he feels like I deserve a greater part of the attention due to my circumstance, or whether he is being guarded. Regardless of why, our conversations always came back around to me. My pain, my experience, what it must feel like to be inactive when activity is everything to you, what it was to be an artist.

The surgery experience is always part of it, but he digs deeper, and most of all he asks to know more. If you ask, I will tell you. Especially when I think you truly care to know. When you don't care, you ask surface questions and do your best to make occasional eye contact to pretend you're paying attention. With his questions, I feel like he is trying to understand what I feel from inside. With his eyes, he lets me know he cares.

He's a writer and asks me to describe the pain with a writer's detail. What is the depth of the pain? What quality does the pain have or does it change? What makes it worse? Is there ever any relief? What are the effects of it? The precision he requests from my answers are an exercise for me. Labeling seems to give me the opportunity to simultaneously characterize what I am feeling and ever so slightly detach from it. I have to tune in further to find the right words, but once I say them, it becomes information that exists outside my body and I am able to let go of a small part of the experience of them.

He has a deep curiosity about my experience as an artist. I try to draw out the reasons I think he could consider himself an artist, but I know all too well the feeling of considering yourself a fraud with that word. But he respects my creativity and reminds me that that's as much of a part of who I am as my physicality. How can he know these things about me after such a short time? Why does it feel like he can see through me?

He is compassionate, and when I try to brush off how scared I am about my future, he seems to know better. Every once in awhile I glance over, and he's looking at me with eyes that have taken on a seriousness and intensity, melting away my armor. It's as if his hands are on my cheeks directing me to look in his eyes as he's saying, *look at me, are you listening? I believe in you. You can do this. I don't care if you recognize your own strength, I recognize it, and I believe in you.*

Trusted advisor

His ability to draw out the depth of my experience then meet it with the perfect mixture of tenderness and concern has given my vulnerability a safe place to occupy. My mom is the only other person who has been completely intertwined in the every day struggles and triumphs of my initial recovery. I rely on them both to be my advisors when I feel my own vision is clouded.

<u>Text conversation - December 5th, 2011</u>

Conflicting emotions are having a battle inside my guts and I'm not a fan. Not concentrating well.

What's the latest? Any news on healing, or just getting sick of it?

Rescheduled my six week post op for this Thursday instead of next. They could let me walk at that point, or it could be too soon and who knows when we reevaluate. I'm just nervous and making myself panic.

Ooooh. Early huh? Well in my opinion, which I might not have a right to offer, you should make sure it's fully healed...and I know you will, just thinking. But don't panic whatever you do! :)

Don't worry, it has nothing to do with what I want. They won't let me walk til I'm ready.

Ah well then. Sending calm, good thoughts to your brain and your hip.

Who knew all this small stuff would break me when I've already come this far.

You're not broken. I'd guess you're going through some pretty understandable stuff, worries and annoyance at not having any control.

And I wanted to show him I was strong.

<u>Text conversation - December 8th, 2011</u>

I can walk!!!!!! Still need extra support for that leg because it's like a noodle, but it's a start!

Holy shit that's awesome!! How does it feel, what did they say?

Feels creepy. He says no restrictions just use discretion. It's all healing really well. Can't believe you left town for my big moment!

I'm sorry, I'm happy for you! Congratulatory drink is in order.

And his words of confidence made the success feel that much sweeter.

Text conversation - December 10th, 2011

> *How's your hip and that left leg?*

Hip feels fine. Legs and back are super fatigued. My walk has drastically improved since Thursday though!

> *I'd say that's all good news. Limp?*

Big time. I tried to gangsta it up, :) though not necessarily effectively. I even do pretty well at stairs and will hopefully move back to my room soon!

> *I knew you'd kick ass recovering.*

Back on the outside

December 17th, 2011

    I have only been walking for a little more than a week and it's a lovely winter day so am meeting up with Kalen to go for an official walk on Mount Tabor, a gorgeous hilltop park that overlooks the city. We meet at his house and when I first walk in he is stunned at how well I am walking. I have a pretty serious limp, but aside from that am doing quite well. When we get in the car, he reaches over and squeezes my leg. I take it as non-verbal communication that he's proud of me, and it feels good. I feel proud of myself as well. He has seen me progress from the hospital bed, to needing help getting into my own bed, to using the walker, to using crutches, and now I'm officially walking on my own!

    We arrive at Mt. Tabor and he's still protectively concerned for me as we make our way up a decent number of stairs. Strolling, albeit extraordinarily slowly, down the path feels so good! It's nice to be out in the air again, and after months of being highly sedentary, the stair climb has my heart pumping at a higher rate than usual. We sit on a bench looking out at the city and talk. His nervous twitch is back, more than usual, and things feel a little awkward, though I look straight past it. My claustrophobia about being limited in my participation with the world seems to be dissipating into the crisp winter air. I feel my life force regaining strength with the opportunity to get back in action, to reshape my direction. Having Kalen next to me makes me feel strong enough to face the challenges ahead.

    As we drive back, my brain can't help but entertain thoughts of being able to take a lazy afternoon nap with him, cuddle with him, take the emotional bond we have established, and see where it goes. I'm finally free, finally not broken, this feels like the beginning.

When we get to his house, it's as if a shock of cold air just blew into the room, it feels icy. He doesn't sit next to me this time. The conversation vanishes and we're like strangers with nothing to say. I'm on the big couch by myself while he sits in the chair across the room. My gut is telling me to just stand up and walk out, but I can't bring myself to do it. I want to know what's going on, but perhaps I already do. I feel it. It's the fear I haven't allowed myself to acknowledge. My sense is that reality has slowly set in, and he's realized he isn't comfortable with it. Here I am sitting in his house, no longer the imaginary friend whom he could visit at his convenience. Now I'm a girl who wants to be a part of his life, introduced to his friends, have a place.

He finally sits beside me, and I let my head fall on his shoulder. I don't want him to see my eyes. I mumble, unsure if I'm meaning to say it out loud, "You tricked me." He gets uncomfortable, and requests to know what I mean. I have nothing else to say. From my guts I know it is true. His half of the connection we had just melted away and I can feel it. He isn't ready to have me in his life. He doesn't want me there. He talks about freedom that he's not ready to give up. The familiar numbness of shock and denial spreads across my brain. I have no recollection of what else was said during that conversation, all that remains is the heaviness of knowing, but not understanding.

No spark

Over the next couple months things begin to change. Our interactions are more infrequent, and mostly just make me feel sad about the loss of what I thought I knew, and incredibly insecure that I have nothing to offer after all. I cry. A lot. I feel anger. Both at him for being so careless with someone so fragile, and at the fact that relationships require both halves to feel the same way and all I had control over was the 50 percent I brought to the table. I perceived it one way. He perceived it another way. We shared the experience, but each through our own eyes.

Emerging from months of physical pain, I am now experiencing another kind of pain. I try to sit with the discomfort as I have been practicing endlessly. But perhaps, just like my hip pain, there is an understandable answer. After weeks of miserable contemplation about what to do, I hope asking for honesty will help me see what changed, what is missing. Then, I hope I am strong enough to hear the answer.

Email message - February 6th, 2012
There's nothing tangible 'missing', you have no drawbacks in my eyes, no check boxes unchecked; I just don't feel the spark I want to feel. I know it when I feel it.

Intermission

Journal Entry - December 31st, 2011
2011 was quite possibly the most challenging year of my life. I experienced a level of sadness that I'd never known before contrasted with an immense amount of love and support.

It's tempting to try to grasp tightly to those things that bring joy and make you feel good, especially when they come following some particularly dark moments. My own personal hope for 2012 is to be able to recognize the impermanence of both joy and sadness, be consumed by neither, and find peace in the balance that comes with fluctuation.

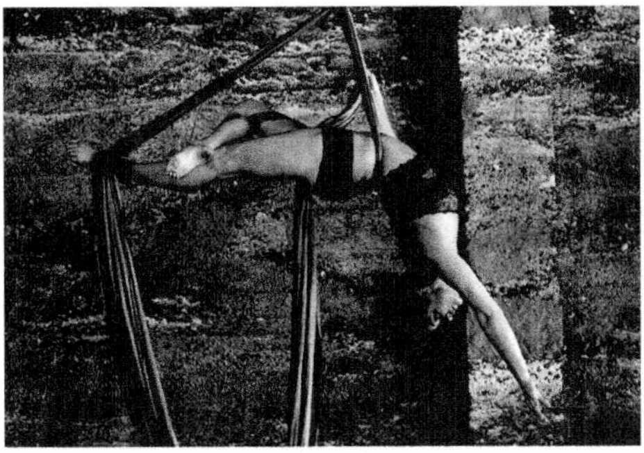
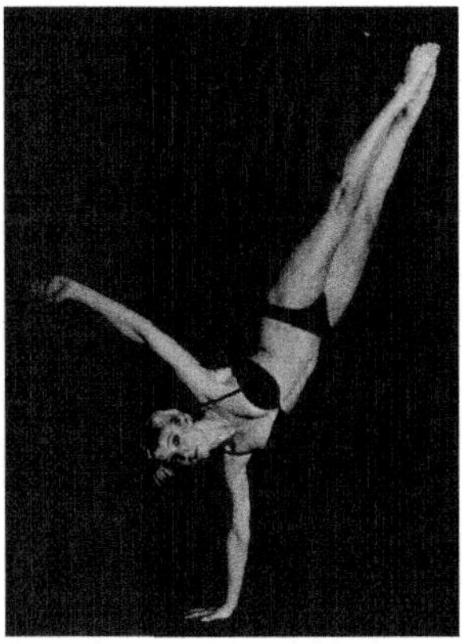
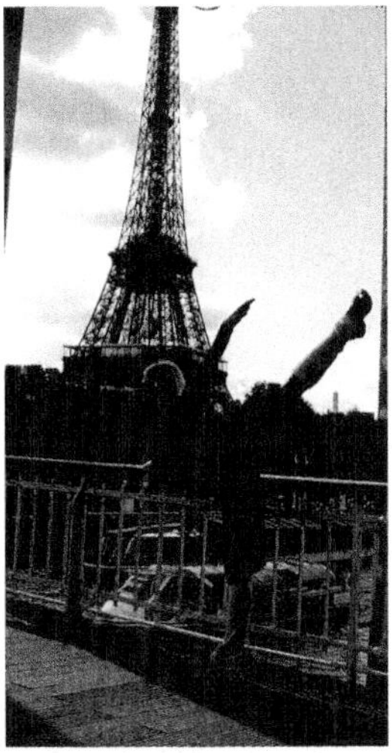
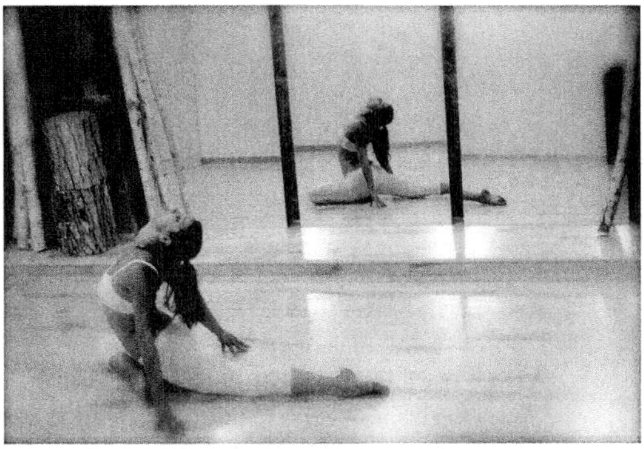
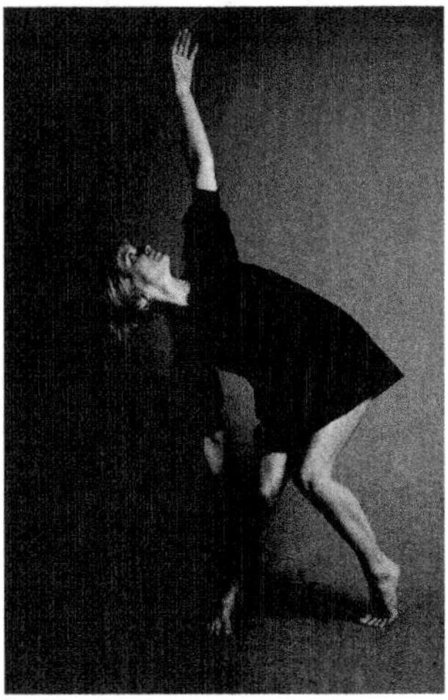
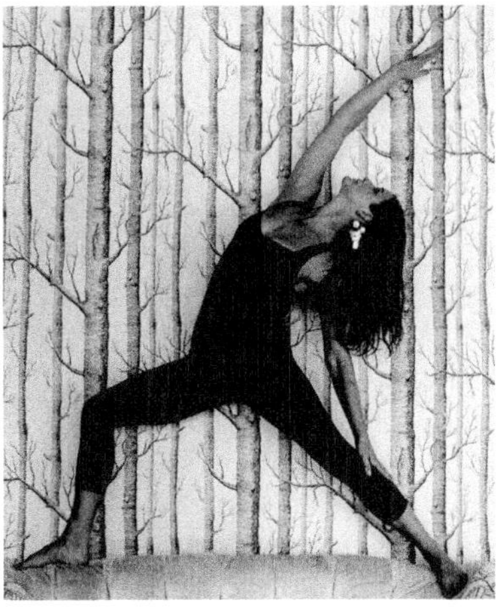

124

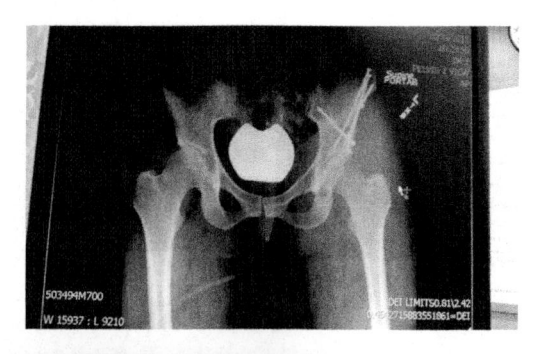

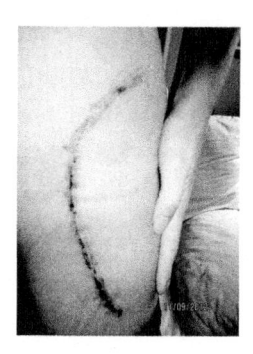

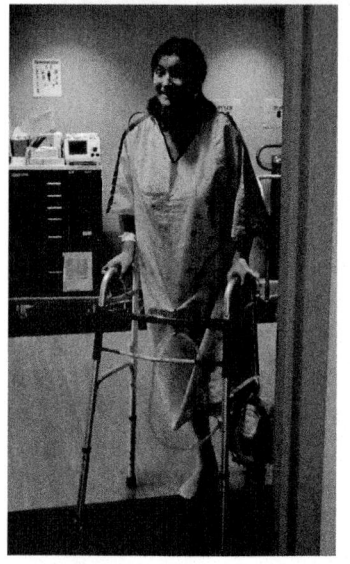

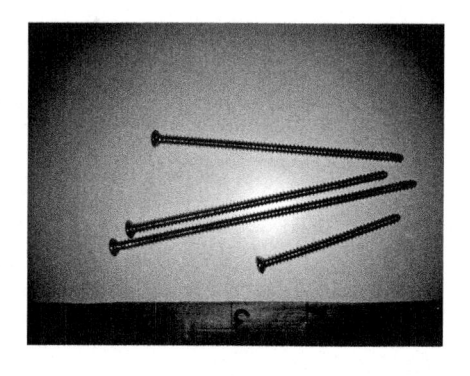

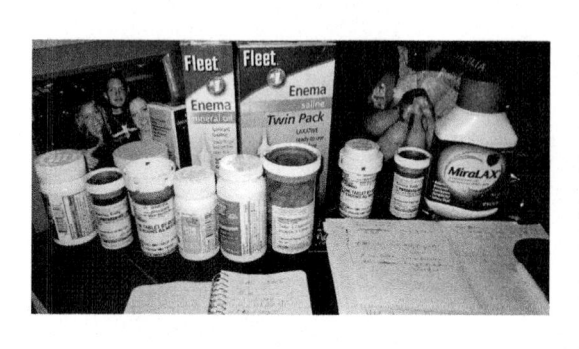

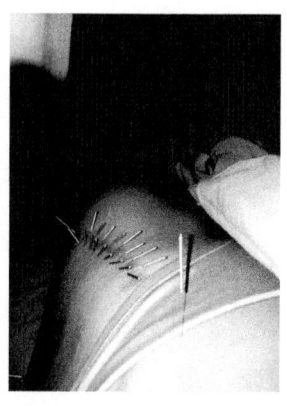

Part Seven

The flabby tin man

I got the go ahead to walk less than a week ago and am already eager to test my body. Dr. Holt said my bone is fully healed so I don't have any restrictions there. The labrum will actually take twelve weeks to heal fully, so I have another six weeks to go. I shouldn't be in too much danger of impeding that process with my activities, considering the natural limitations I'll be working with due to not using the muscles for six weeks. I still plan to use my one crutch if I will be on my feet for longer periods or have further to walk, though my current max is about the equivalent of two blocks.

Mom took to to calling me the flabby tin man (flattering I know) because I'm exceptionally stiff, but also because I lost 15 pounds, mainly of muscle, so am mostly just a skeleton holding up a bunch of saggy flesh. Ok, I don't look that horrific, but I can't say I look good. It was immediately clear with my first steps that atrophy had temporarily claimed all abilities my left leg previously possessed. My leg was so weak that I was not able to put my full weight on it as it may collapse underneath me. Nor could I bend at the hip, or at the knee beyond a few degrees. Clearly, this means still finding modifications for everyday activities.

I must continue to use my hands to lift my leg into bed and in the car. Those have become habit anyway, so I don't really think much of it and they feel like minor adjustments. Some of my other inconveniences, however, may be more extreme. For example, I had my cousin and his friend move my bed back upstairs to my room. The complication is, I'm not quite capable of doing the stairs as one usually would. With my leg partially incapacitated, and using my crutch on the narrow staircase with no railing seeming too precarious, I've taken to using my arms to bear crawl on all fours up the stairs and crab walk down. While it's funny looking, it's perfectly functional and allows me to be back in my room, so totally worth it. Depending on how you look at it, the more desperate adjustments represent either my impatience, or my intense motivation to return to normal life.

Aside from the left leg that will need focused work, I am anxious to see how the other three quarters of my body will bounce back. Last night I tried to recreate some familiar Pilates moves and yoga poses which resulted in some interesting discoveries. Lying on my back, I attempted what are called knee folds in Pilates where, with your knees bent and feet flat on the floor, you alternately lift one knee and the other while tapping the opposite toe to the mat. Not too long into that I started feeling nauseated. Lifting the left leg felt awkward, difficult, and generally uneasy. Moving on. I decided to try some core work in which my legs were static. While totally weak and incredibly stiff, the muscles appeared to be functioning still, so it felt like progress. On to some yoga. I considered child's pose, yet quickly realized that my inability to bend at the hip and the knee ruled that out completely. Needing to be a bit more creative, I navigated my way into downward dog, placed my head on the floor, and gently pressed into an awkward version of a headstand. Success! Adrenaline elevated, I tried a few other moves that didn't require the use of my leg, and for the most part those went well too. Unbelievable, and what a relief! In my mind I had been imagining the rest of my body being as decrepit as my leg, so headstands were not at all what I visualized this stage looking like. I suppose I had been preparing for worst case scenario all along and so far, things were unfolding well toward the best case scenario side of the spectrum.

My spirits are up a bit now that my daily activities aren't quite as daunting, and I can actually begin to work on the recovery part.

Two timing

Knowing the physical therapy portion of my recovery could dramatically change the outcome, I wanted to be sure I was working with someone who understood the physical needs of a dancer. I found two therapists whose reputations were promising, and I tried them both. I felt a little guilty about two timing my therapists, but I'm glad I did.

The first one I went to seemed nice enough. She appeared knowledgeable and understanding about my goals. I brought in my op report since the surgery I had is uncommon, and I thought it would be helpful for her to see in accurate medical terms what occurred during the procedure. When I came in the second time she asked questions that were blatantly stated on my op report, indicating to me she hadn't read it. She also put me on a stationary bike right away. As we were walking towards it, I mentioned that I hadn't been able to bike for many years prior as it was specifically aggravating to my hips and caused a high degree of pain. She didn't seem too concerned, put me on the bike, told me how many minutes to be there, then walked back to her room leaving me alone on the bike. I stopped pedaling immediately once she left the room and waited my assigned minutes before getting off. For the rest of the appointment, I continued to ask questions about the physical therapy process, though her answers were brief and our conversation kept being redirected to more social topics.

Luckily, my other choice contrasted that experience greatly and gave me no question as to who to continue with for PT. Maria read my op report before entering the room and had a short discussion about it before we began. I told her I wanted to understand the healing process better, allowing me to be very active in my own recovery. She obliged by narrating what she was doing and why throughout the treatment, as well as bringing in a model pelvis on occasion to help solidify my understanding. Each session was 45 minutes of manual work followed by 30 minutes with an assistant doing exercises.

Journal Entry - January 4th, 2012
Deep stinging pain in the hip bone... hope I'm not getting ahead of my recovery.

Perpetual nausea

January 10th, 2012

  I arrive at PT and am taken back to a private room where I change into a pair of purple shorts and lie down on the table. When Maria comes in, she asks how things have been going since the last appointment, which varies greatly from day to day. Some days I get to report about a new progression or redeeming moment, but today I am mostly concerned with how stiff I feel, and some pain I'm unable to identify. The scar tissue feels nearly solid, and when I try to lift my knee, it's as if a golf ball is lodged into my hip flexor preventing further motion. The pain I'm experiencing feels like stinging and is right at my hip bone.

  She begins by working on the range of motion of my hip joint. Usually this entails her placing the back of my knee on her shoulder, using both hands to traction my femur, then trying to work a little give into my joint capsule. She repeatedly tests how far my knee comes to my chest, hoping for advancements in the angle.

  The nervous feeling that something isn't quite right washes over me. It's not that I actually think something is wrong, it's just a feeling my body gets during almost every treatment session. The sensation is more dulled when we're working on motions where my knee bends off to the side. But when she tries to bring my knee directly to my chest or across the body, the feeling is more panicky. On the inside my body is screaming, *No no no! That's not right!* She asks me to describe my level of discomfort, yet it's hard to distinguish the unwelcome from the unfamiliar. Since my proprioception is not accustomed to my new alignment, my body sometimes sends alarm messages to my brain during perfectly safe movements it's just not used to.

  After spending some time with the joint capsule we do some work on the scar tissue. Maria says, "I'm going to go grab the ASTYM™ tools, I'll be right back," and just those words are enough to generate a grimace. ASTYM™ involves scraping the scar tissue with a small plastic tool. As she runs the tool strategically around the pocket scar over the front of my hip, the texture of the tissue feels like Rice Krispies underneath my skin. That's the scar tissue that we are trying to break up. The worst is when she goes near the screw head protruding from the bone. I'm writhing on the table. Her face is in a grimace as well. She says she can feel all the crunchiness vibrate back up into her hands. We have a lot to work through. My adductor (a muscle that extends along the inner thigh from the groin to the knee) is the next victim of this vicious tool. My adductor has been in protection mode for years trying to prevent my bones from rubbing together and has refused to release its intense grip. As she pressed the tool into my flesh, pushing it down from my knee towards my groin, I squeeze my eyes shut, hold my breath, and clench my fists. Maria promises we are almost done, just a few more times like that. We are both eager to move past this part. While that portion of the treatment only lasts about five minutes, it's one of the most gut-wrenching experiences. As soon as she's finished she has me stand up and walk around. The difference feels night and day. My body finally feels able to move freely again, the stiffness so dramatically reduced by the scraper, it makes it worth it. Maria also reminds me that my op report indicated they literally cut off my hip bone to gain access to the other cuts, and suggests that my pain is probably quite normal considering.

    The nauseated feeling lingers for the better portion of the day.

Crutches at the gym

About twice a week following work at White Bird, I go to the gym to use the pool. It is the lowest impact option I have to feel like I'm getting a real work out. The walk from the parking lot to the gym, to the changing room, and to the pool, is far enough that I still prefer to use my crutches. Needless to say, I get a lot of strange looks, when I crutch in the door.

I had been swimming a couple times a week prior to surgery to keep myself as strong and fit as possible. The contrast of my ability now to before is considerable. Half way through one lap, I feel like I'm about to sink to the bottom. I've developed a routine where I walk the length of the pool, then swim one length, and continue to alternate. During my walking laps I include multiple variations. Using the support of the water, I am able to lift my knee higher than I can on land, so practice a high kneed walk. I also walk backwards and do side steps to target different muscle groups and angles of movement. Near the end, I incorporate some water ballet. The water acts simultaneously as a support and resistance, and I hope to get my dance muscles back to some reasonable level of conditioning.

When I get out of the pool, I can't help but be self-conscious of my deep purple shark bite. The scar looks precisely like you'd imagine it would if it a shark had ferociously clamped its jaws around my hip eager for the taste of a human drumstick. When I think about it like that it seems a bit more badass, yet with no story attached, it is simply ugly and frightening. Though far from bikini season, I know I will have to come to own this mark with pride of what I've lived through. My planned response to inevitable curiosity is something like, *You should see the shark!*

A halfway new experience in yoga

January 22nd, 2012

  Sometime in November when I was laid up, there was a Groupon offering $30 for a month of unlimited yoga classes. Since it didn't expire for nine months or so, I decided to buy it, dreaming about the day I'd be able to get back to my practice.

  Today is my first day back, and I have no idea what to expect. I've been going to physical therapy for about a month now and trying things out here and there to check in with my abilities. A full 90 minute yoga class, however, the content of which I have no control over, and which is not geared toward rehabbing patients, is a different story. I chose to go to Vinyasa as that's what my body is most familiar with, though I know I will need to find modifications for many things. I just don't know exactly what yet.

  Class begins and we start in Child's Pose which I've already established I can't do. I can't even make a similar shape so I just sit on my block with my eyes closed. As we gradually move into the flow, it is luckily going at a slow enough pace for me to keep up. Since the hip socket has been rotated laterally, my femur and the muscles surrounding don't understand how to flex my hip. The straightforward motion of trying to draw my knee towards my chest results in my knee pulling off to the side as if trying to follow the path of my original positioning. I am able to make sense of that during simple movement patterns, but progressing into more complex movements my brain and my body have a harder time working together.

  A common transition from Downward Dog into the Warrior poses is to lift the leg up behind you and then step the foot between the hands. My right side is pretty much exactly as it was before. The left side I have neither the strength nor the ability to bend my hip to bring the knee towards my chest. I get my foot half way there, though significantly off to the side, and have to lift it the rest of the way with my hand. Once in Warrior 1 on the left side, basically a lunge where your back heel swivels into a slight external rotation to reach the floor, I struggle to find my alignment. In this pose, the ribcage is supposed to face forward, and on the right side that's exactly what it feels like it's doing. On the left however, my torso feels like it's in an intense twist trying to face front. The teacher walks by and I whisper to her to check my alignment. She says it looks fine, to which I conclude that what my Warrior 1 used to feel like is not what it's going to feel like anymore.

Continuing through my practice, single leg balances on my left leg, like Warrior 3 or Half Moon, feel equally crazy. Not only is my leg still extraordinarily weak, but it still doesn't feel quite like my own. It takes nerves a full year to grow back and my quadricep is still numb and tingly. During surgery, they had to cut only one muscle, the TFL (Tensor Fasciae Latae), and it's possible that the nerves involved in that cut won't return and I will never regain full feeling down the side of my leg. It's a long way to go before that mile marker, so I will just have to do my best with it for now. Finally wrapping up the flow, we move into inversions, twists, backbends, and then Savasana (Corpse Pose).

Upon leaving class, I feel good. The once familiar movements weren't wildly out of reach, and I was simply happy that I could attend class. I knew there were many things that I would need to work on, but feel a sense of acceptance for the long road ahead.

One hour after class, my whole body felt like it had been hooked up to an electrical stimulator. It was as if each and every cell was vibrating riotously inside my body, and I was suddenly slammed with exhaustion. I went to bed at 8:00 pm.

Journal Entry - January 23rd, 2012
My yoga experience yesterday has me a bit concerned. I am wondering if my brain was so distracted with taking it all in that the

physical effects of the practice were delayed? If this is the case, I need to be cautious with how I proceed with my physical activities. I am reminded of the words of Dr. Keating warning me that the most common cause of recovery complications in athletes is due to trying to return to a high level too quickly. I am determined to avoid that.

15 weeks

I'm 15 weeks past surgery, yet it's hard to know what that even means. During the initial six weeks post surgery, despite the fact that I couldn't walk, go up or down stairs, stand up in the shower, or use my own muscles to lift my leg in and out of the car, recovery mode felt more logical. Of course there's a healing period, my pelvis is broken! Being decrepit was an obvious reality proved by my use of a walker. I now seem to be experiencing a more confusing part of recovery where I have to make choices about my level of physicality and my compromised abilities that are no longer plain to see.

If I didn't take some amount of pride in my physical ability I wouldn't have chosen the profession that I did. Consequently, being weaker than what I am used to, or unable to participate because I physically can't is humbling. Recently, I went out on my first hike post surgery. I know the trail well and it's not particularly steep or challenging. Hardly half way in to my planned route, maybe a mile at most, I suddenly couldn't go any further. My hips seemed to have twisted out of place and my Sacroiliac joint was producing a sharp pain. I sat down off to the side of the trail only to discover that that wasn't at all comfortable, so instead, I gently lay down. Trying my best to look like I was just having a pleasantly reflective moment, some other hikers passed by and asked if I was okay. I assured them I was, though once they left wondered if I would soon be hoping some other hikers would come by and ask again in case I would have to endure the humiliation of needing help out. Luckily, once the pain settled down I was able to stand up and walk back out to my car. While that incident wasn't at all unreasonable due to my circumstances, I couldn't help but feel defeated and lame.

The flip side of this involves a very different story. At some point, not too distant in time from my hiking debacle, I was demonstrating something in my Adidas Pilates class and one woman exclaimed, "How is it that you just went through major hip surgery and can still do this exercise better than I ever have in my life!" The truth is, there is a very clear answer to that. I can do it because I have been training and conditioning my muscles many hours a week for years. The reason is similar to why I was able to do a headstand three days after being approved to walk. Both movements do not challenge my restrictions, and I have a strong base of muscle memory for them. Whereas she had not yet mastered the move to begin with, I had. Despite what my body had gone through, I was able to find that ability again because I had already taken the time to develop the skill and coordination to accomplish it. As a side note, an athlete does not compare their abilities to that of the general population, they compare to the best in their field, and in that sense I am not even in the ball park.

What I'm beginning to realize is that despite my many accomplishments and regained abilities, I still feel heavily depressed because I'm still stuck in an uncertain transition mode and still not feeling like "me" yet. In my early diagnosis stage, I felt immense conflict between what I could do versus what I should do, all in the context of what I was willing to compromise. Currently, I feel like I'm in the same boat, just painted a different color. And that boat, regardless what color, remains floating in a sea of depression.

The no end in sight black sea

<u>Journal Entry - February 10th</u>
I usually think of myself as a strong person, but I haven't been lately. I've been impatient with time, I've been too dependent on other people and I've generally just lost perspective about the bigger picture. I have no idea where to go from here.

Confusion, anxiety, depression, helplessness, and fear are all emotions associated with trauma, and while my official traumatic incident is in the past, it seems like those emotions remain lurking in my body. Any small obstacle, minor heartbreak, or change of plans, is suddenly magnified into a cyclone of irrational emotion.

Potentially, the worst thing about being depressed is, it feels like an automatic failure. I don't know how other people feel about experiencing their emotions, but I know for myself that path has been indirect and fraught with confusion. In childhood we have the luxury of expressing our emotion in its most pure form, whether pounding our fists on the floor in a raging tantrum, sobbing hysterically at a tiny injustice, or giggling in utter joy about who knows what. Regardless, the expression comes out and is more or less accepted as normal. But once we become adults, there's an entire rule book written on what is acceptable, what is normal, and what is appropriate timing. I'm not saying I wish adults were allowed to tantrum, but I do question the societal expectation to mask emotions and be pleasantly optimistic at all times.

Luckily, artists are often famous for being overly emotional, so when the feelings of guilt arise about expressing my emotions, I often console myself by thinking that it's just part of my job of being an artist. Unfortunately, that's not really how it works. When you get riled up people always tell you to calm down, when you're sad people remind you to keep your chin up, when you're going through a tough moment people remind you that others may have it much worse. The last one is my least favorite. Why the comparison? Why am I not allowed to feel how I feel? Why aren't my problems valid unless they are the worst problems anyone has ever experienced in the world??

I honestly don't think I have been pessimistic about my situation. I have felt very concerned, perhaps consumed, and mostly just sad. It's a sadness I can't seem to shake nor see the end of. Almost a year since this whole process began, I still feel the raw, dark emotion as a looming presence just beneath the surface at all times. There is no way to process everything at once, so I try to break it down into more manageable pieces. Yet, each piece seems to have an affect on the all others and I often find myself just as confused as before.

Right around my 30th birthday last August I made an assessment of the various aspects of my life. Alas, six months later I'm still single, still financially insecure, still out of shape, and still uncertain of what my future will look like. The difference now is that I've been at the throat of these struggles long enough that a small amount of acceptance of living with uncertainty is gradually starting to seep in.

Journal Entry - February 21st, 2012
Emotion is powerful, chemical, inevitable and often uncontrollable. Perhaps that's why we're afraid of it. It's also revealing, vulnerable, irrational, and consuming. But it's the human experience and a great deal of beauty can arise from it when we honor its existence.

My Mumford anthem

Already in love with the song "After the Storm" by Mumford And Sons I have begun listening to it every time I feel a tinge of hopelessness. The first two lines of the chorus gently remind me that both the place I'm in, and the tears that pour out, are temporary. Intellectually I know I will get beyond this, I just can't feel it yet. The next lines promise me that one day love will not break me, but keep me safe. This I'm skeptical of. I don't hide from love so I know how sweet it can be. I also know that love and risk go hand in hand. The next few lines point out that there is a block in my view and I have to get past it to see what is there. When I visualize what that might look like, the distance from that place doesn't seem so far away after all. Burdensome, yes, but manageable because a sense of joy will return to my life if I keep working towards it. The final line of the chorus is my biggest challenge. It asks me to approach my journey with grace in my heart. Can I...Am I...? I guess I doubt it, but it does give me something to strive for.

Dove tail

<u>Journal Entry - March 8th, 2012</u>
When they said I'd be non-weight bearing for six to eight weeks I took five and a half. When they said I'd need a crutch or a cane for the month following my return to walking, I took three days before ditching the extra support. Following my go-ahead to move, I went up the stairs day two, did a headstand day three, went back to Vinyasa yoga within a few weeks, and have even started back doing some aerial. Indeed these are things I feel really good about.

But there's another side of healing that's much less tangible. It's the side that includes the mental and emotional healing process. When I was on crutches and/or still visibly "recovering," it made more sense. At this point, if you didn't know I'd had surgery, you wouldn't be able to tell just by looking at me which is requiring me to be humble again. I feel so incapable in comparison to what I could do before. I'm always trying to explain the whole story to people, though I know it's just my pride. What I used to be able to do is irrelevant. What I can do now, and the further progressions I make, are all that count from here on out.

When I get to acupuncture we walk back to the room and Alexis says the same thing she always says: "So what can I do for you today?" I hate it when this happens, mainly because it's happened so many times over the course of my going to her, but today I just start sobbing and can't even speak to answer. There's something about being back in that safe space of her treatment room that makes it impossible to put on the front of being okay when I'm not. I finally am able to snuffle out that I've had a deep feeling of nausea happening right in my solar plexus. In yoga this area is referred to as Manipuraka and is associated with power, will, and identity. Not surprisingly, my insides in this region are feeling tangled.

I always go into acupuncture with a list of about 10 things I need to work on: adductor, scar tissue, femoral nerve, digestion shut down due to stress, and often emotional well-being. Today, there is no question which is my priority. My gut alien is being especially stubborn!

Alexis leaves and allows me to get undressed and under the sheets. The table is heated and feels nice. I spritz a little Deep Detox potion on the pillow before I lie down and try to settle in. Acupuncture has been a life saver throughout this process but it isn't always particularly pleasant in the moment.

I'm willing myself to calm down before Alexis returns. She knocks to be sure I'm ready, then comes in and starts strategically placing needles. My body jumps here and there and I feel sorry that my body still hasn't opened up to this. She apologizes as if it's she that's hurting me, but the hurt is coming from the inside. The next needle she places is in that spot directly below the sternum where the rib cage curtains open around the supple beginning of the belly.

As the needle goes in, my eyes widen and I exclaim, "It felt like you just peeled my ribcage back!" The sensation produces a distinct visual image of my ribcage peeling back, opening up a hole in my center that continues on to a bottomless void. She replies, "Yes, that point is called the Dove Tail and is supposed to feel about like that." She leaves me to rest and the feeling continues for a number of minutes during which I feel tangible tension pouring out of my body and dissipating into nothing.

When she returns to take out my needles and do some body work, the heavy feeling of dread has completely lifted. I walk out of the appointment feeling like a new person.

Squeezed and soaked

Encouraged by my first successful yoga class, I'm eager to incorporate a few classes each week into my routine. I'll build back my strength in no time! Whereas I entered my initial class with concern and hesitation, I plan to attend this and future classes with humility and discipline.

We begin, and I mentally breeze right past my inability to do Child's Pose. There will be plenty more poses, no need to be hung up on that one. Next up is a supine twist, which is always quite luxurious. The Indian yoga guru, B.K.S. Iyengar, uses the term, "squeeze and soak" to describe the benefits of twisting. The compression and subsequent releasing of the organs stimulates blood flow forcing out built up toxins, then allowing fresh blood to circulate in, carrying oxygen and essential nutrients to the tissue. Twists are considered to have a cleansing effect and I'm eager to be cleansed of all my meds as well as stress and emotional toxins.

Gradually moving past the twist, we make our way to standing and begin Sun Salutations. I'm a little torn here. Movement in general feels great, but my forward fold feels wonky and my arms flimsy. Reminder, accept where I'm at. Continuing the flow into Warrior poses. We always begin on the right side. I lift my leg up behind me and step it through, then extend my torso up to Warrior 1. On the left side, I lift my leg up behind me, then gingerly try to step it forward on my mat. Not getting very far, I reach my hand down, clasp my ankle and lift my foot the rest of the way, then hand-over-hand walk my torso up to finally emerge in a rendition of Warrior 1. All Warrior poses on my left feel merely like vague resemblances of what they used to. Repeating this, or similar motions a few times through, I'm fighting back frustration. What used to be a smooth, continuous motion is now broken down into awkward, choppy, and inefficient movements. We finally take a pause in Downward Dog, and I'm blinking back tears. I'm upside down, my face is at least partially hidden, and I let some emotion leak out. By the time we are back up to standing at the top of the mat, I've pulled it together.

Whereas last time the effects of movement felt energizing, this time the blood circulating through my veins feels murky. Exhaustion is setting in already and the mental approach I had intended in my practice, is slipping away. With 45 minutes to go I attempt to shut down my brain entirely, yet it's rapidly shuffling thoughts in every direction making it nearly impossible to rein them in. Deep breaths seem to feed the fire of anxiety, triggering the churning deep in my gut.

After what felt like an eternally long class, I arrive in Savasana half-heartedly trying to hush my softly audible sobs. My body has been taken over and it's much easier to surrender helplessly to the demons that need to emerge than to stifle them. I roll up my mat and try to slip out of class without having to make eye contact with anyone.

My body was awake

I don't want to give the wrong impression that I'm using aggression to move forward with my recovery. That's not it at all. There's bound to be resistance throughout this process, though I truly believe I'm not forcing myself to do things I'm not ready for, nor setting excessively high expectations. On the other hand, the exact boundary where I could potentially push too far and cross into danger mode isn't completely clear.

I was having a conversation recently with my dear friend Syann, who is both a dancer and a yoga teacher. I was explaining to her that I'm trying to listen to my body, but it's sending many messages and acting very capricious sometimes. My challenges with yoga and the accompanying meltdowns of emotion for example, seem within reason as this is a sensitive process. During acupuncture, my muscles often involuntarily pull away or react with hostility to both needles and body work. I mentally remind myself that while it's unpleasant, the treatment is meant to heal me and I continue to categorize it under necessary-steps-toward-recovery. What I don't understand, however, is how a simple hug from a friend can create potent feelings of unease. How my personal space bubble has tripled in size and I am more comfortable when people aren't physically too close to me or in contact with me. These are the experiences I am not able to make sense of rationally.

Syann pointed out that while anesthesia caused my brain to be unaware during the procedure, my body was awake and experiencing what was going on. Here's what my body witnessed:

<u>Operation Report (condensed):</u>
Epidural was placed. Patient was transferred to the operating room. General anesthesia was administered....

Surface landmarks were identified and an incision was made for an anterior approach to the hip and pelvic brim. The tensor fascia was incised laterally, and the muscle fibers reflected laterally....The periosteum over the pelvic brim was incised, and subperiosteal dissection was carried medially down the inner table of the pelvis...The anterior superior iliac spine was osteotomized...The reflected head of the rectus was identified and detached...This allowed wide anterior exposure of the capsule...the ischium was palpated with curved Mayo scissors.

We then turned our attention to the pubic osteotomy...blunt retractors were placed while the osteotomy was made with a saw...The final posterior column osteotomy was then made using a series of osteotomes, all under direct fluoroscopic guidance, to meet up with the inferior ischial cut...

...The correction was then held provisionally with K-wires...until we were satisfied with the position....we then exchanged K-wires for fully-threaded cortical screws...Fixation was achieved with a single anterior to posterior home run screw and 3 superior to inferior screws through the iliac wing...

...With the osteotomy complete and correction obtained and fixed, we then set about the intra-articular portion of the procedure. The anterior capsule was again exposed...The labrum was largely intact in the periphery; however, it was hypertrophic and detached at the base in a bucket-handle fashion from approximately 9 o'clock to 12 o'clock. The margins of the detachment were freshened with a 10 blade....The acetabular rim was then debrided back to a bony bed using angled curettes and pituitary rongeurs. We then fixed the labrum with suture anchors...The hip was taken through range of motion...

...The wound was copiously irrigated and then closed in layers in a cosmetic fashion...Prior to final closure fluoroscopic views were obtained to check the correction and again ensure none of the hardware was intra-articular....

During surgery my body became a construction zone with saws and screws, scissors, and blades. While my brain was blissfully under the influence of medication, I wasn't a corpse! I was alive with breath flowing, a heart beating, blood circulating. Seeing the picture in this light suddenly gave me a rushing sense of compassion for my body as simply a living being. Previously, I had been focusing on the external factors, my knee to chest angle, regaining physical independence, the timeline of when I'd be dancing again. Within the whirlwind of my mind stacking on a new list of goals as soon as I'd accomplished the original, I neglected to seek peace with my body who had witnessed, processed, and held this trauma within my cells.

I now plan to move forward with a completely new sense of the whole picture.

Change in strategy

I am officially entering a new stage which I have titled, "The Positive Reinforcement Stage." When I think about it, external factors of time or money or physically not being willing to stop doing what I was doing, have often won over actually taking care of my body. The conundrum of this is curious. While a high degree of physical performance is essential to both my soul and my livelihood, those are the exact two things that kept me from finding a solution for so long. But now that I've found new work and am on the other side of surgery knowing it went well, I can reassess my relationship with many of those components.

For whatever reason, my visualization of recovery looked more feeble and pathetic for much longer than has been the reality. Instead, I have been able to witness how phenomenal the body's healing powers are, which has has been incredibly encouraging and even empowering. My ability to be patient with the physical recovery timeline is much easier with the worst-case-scenario possibility off the table.

Financially, while I'm still clearly behind from the goal I had barely reached pre-surgery, and where I would have hoped to be at upon entering my 30's, I have to acknowledge why I'm here. I haven't been sitting lazily around hoping for the world to bring me fame and riches. As part of the bigger picture this is a bump in the road, that will set me behind, but I will bounce back from it. Between insurance, financial assistance from OHSU coming through, the benefit, and a generous family, I am again far from worst-case-scenario. Quite the opposite, I'm extraordinarily blessed and most definitely aware and appreciative of it.

I won't lie. It takes work to continue to feel okay with these things even though I can logically accept them, but even an occasional sense of being at peace with it all is progress.

Now about that healing. I've transitioned to taking Yin Yoga which is restorative in nature. It's meant to open up the connective tissue, fortifying its strength and elasticity. In Yin you use blankets and blocks to support your body in various folds and twists so you are not using muscular effort, allowing gravity to gradually elongate the fibers. The areas of my body that were immobile for six weeks have likely built up some adhesions and could use some gentle encouragement. I've gone to a few classes so far and overall it's feeling good. During one class I had to excuse myself to the restroom in the middle to let some emotion out. But as soon as I did, it didn't linger; like a wave that built up, it crashed and then slipped quietly away.

I have also taken to buying as many massages through Groupon as possible. A $30 massage seems fairly justifiable on any occasion. Unlike physical therapy, which continues to be intense and emotionally exhausting, when I go in for a massage I tell them I'm looking for positive reinforcement for my body...and to not be alarmed by the shark bite.

Invisible separation

I'm back at AWOL working out by myself. The company started rehearsing their annual April show, "Left of Center," back in late December. As I could hardly walk at the time, it would be another show I watched from the audience. We rehearse in a 10,000 square foot warehouse with 30 foot ceilings that is impossible to heat very well, so I haven't been too sad to be missing out on three evenings a week of rehearsals this time of year. But I do feel distanced from the group, which is tough because they're my best friends and I miss the day-to-day silliness that occurs. There's endless dialogue and banter that goes on as well as funny moments when someone trips on the safety mat or looks completely ridiculous while learning a new move. We should make a whole movie out of our bloopers - let's just say, a polished show has inevitably been through many progressions before it arrived there.

It's a challenge to explain the dynamic of our company to someone who isn't involved. The company has had little to no turnover since I started working with them four years ago. We spend nine to twelve hours a week together rehearsing year round, and as many as 40 hours per week during show weeks. We also go on yearly planning retreats to the coast and have had other shows where we are out of town together for the weekend. I point this out because there's a level of intimacy that is bound to develop when you travel with people or spend that much time together. We are all too comfortable talking about bodily functions openly with each other, we can tell someone's mood before they even speak, and we have a stockpile of a million memorable moments spent together.

You would wonder how it's possible that 12 women actually get along that well and it truly is incredible that we do. The bond is somewhere between family, friend, and intimate relationship. The love we have for each other is unconditional and even through disagreements and hurt feelings, there is always a deep sense of care for every member of the group.

The hours in rehearsal are both ridiculously fun and highly intense. On the one hand, we feel completely at home being foolish and having a good time. On the other, we have to merge creative ideas, work with each other physically, and even trust each other with our lives on many occasions. You can't really say that for many professions, which is another thing that makes our bond unique.

So despite the cold weather and daunting challenge of rebuilding my strength, I've been trying to go in one to two times per week to do my own workout in hopes of being reasonably strong by the time we start working on "Art in the Dark," our annual August show.

The big warehouse is divided out into smaller sections. When you walk in the door you are back stage of the main stage. Then you walk along the side of the main stage coming to the audience set up facing it. Adjacent to the audience is an alternate stage with a squishy mat floor that is removed during shows to become the concession area. Tonight as I come in, the company is rehearsing for the show on the main stage. Everyone says "hi" to me, then continues working. I walk over to the alternate stage and start my workout.

I always used to tell my students that the best way to progress is to take baby steps. If you can't do a pull-up for example, you have to find a middle step because you can't go from zero to pull-up with nothing in between. You could jump into it so your chin is above the bar and the elbows begin bent, then let gravity assist the action on the way down. Or you could find a way to support some of your weight so you don't have to lift all of it. Usually just a small assist is all it takes. Regardless of method, if you're not strong enough to pull yourself up, you need to baby step your way there.

In putting my own advice into action, I've created a chart of some strength training exercises and flexibility measurements so I can start where I am, and instead of being frustrated with not being at my highest level, be proud of the progress I'm making. Each week I try to add one more repetition of each exercise. One more is usually pretty easy to mentally wrap my mind around and it's still progress that I can write on my chart. Luckily, my housemate has a pull-up bar set up at the house so I was able to maintain enough of that strength to do four pull-ups. My pre-surgery max was six. I write four down on my chart and move on to some other aerial specific exercises. Tucks (while hanging from the trapeze you pull your knees up to your chest), eight. Then beats (a swing back and forth where on each peak you try to get the body horizontal to the ground), eight. In a class I would usually ask students to do ten of each of these, so eight for me at this point doesn't feel too bad. Straddle beats (same as beats but ending in an inverted straddle at the front peak) are on my list as well, though my sitting straddle has less than a 45 degree angle so doing them on the trapeze isn't accessible yet as my legs wouldn't clear the bar. I rest in between sets and watch what's happening on the main stage.

After trapeze I move on to fabric. First, one straight climb to the top. Then a Russian variation climb to the top. Both are taking a great deal of effort and the length of my resting intervals increases. Tuck inverts (holding on to the fabric in mid-air, bringing the knees to the chest then inverting hips over head), five. Straddle inverts (same as tuck but keeping the legs straight and ending in an up-side-down straddle) but alas I can only do about three, from the floor, with my left leg feeling like a broken wing. When I try to keep my left leg straight and lift it up it feels like a 20 pound weight is attached to my ankle.

Since I get progressively more discouraged throughout the course of any given work out, I have a hard time motivating on my own. With fatigue setting in I call it a day. Walking past the main stage bustling with productivity, I slip out the door and drive home in the rain.

Screws

Dr. Holt told me that he could take my screws out in a simple day procedure if I determined that was necessary. He didn't expect it would be necessary, as most people don't require their screws to come out. But I am not most people, illustrated primarily by reason three in my top three reasons why they need to come out:

1. My physical therapist has a theory that the scar tissue we gruesomely take the scraping tools to each week is perpetually redeveloping due to rubbing against the screw head that sticks out of my hip bone.
2. Said screw head also makes all prone yoga poses feel like I'm getting stabbed, a sensation I feel even while lying on my stomach in bed.
3. The trapeze and hoop are not agreeing with my hardware, as my body violently rejects the two coming in contact which can be a danger on many levels.

No go (go figure)

I call in to set up my appointment. I let the receptionist know that I had surgery about six months ago and am now ready to get the surgical screws taken out. I assure her that I had spoken to Dr. Holt about it in my six week post op appointment and he said it would be no problem. She schedules me for 3:20 pm on Monday, March 15th. This surprises me because he used to be scheduled in the clinic on that day. I ask her to confirm a few things for me to know how to prepare.

Do I need to shower with antibacterial soap and refrain from eating and drinking? How long will it take, and will I need someone to drive me home? She says no to all of the above questions and says to just show up.

Dr. Holt did say it would be a quick day procedure, but I have a hard time imagining he's just going to take a power drill to my hip in his office. But there is no question I was clear about what I scheduled when I spoke to the receptionist, so I write it off as the continued ridiculousness of the system. I've given up on knowing each detail before it happens.

March 15th comes along and I go to the appointment. When I check in at the front, they request x-rays, to which I respond, "I don't actually think I need x-rays today, I'm just here to get my screws out." Confusion crosses the face of the receptionist and she makes a few phone calls. Finally, I'm called back to see Dr. Holt only to discover that indeed this procedure would require antibacterial soap, fasting, and a ride home, as well as a formal pre-op appointment with the anesthesiologist, and a visit to the hospital.

Second time's a charm

Second surgery, Take Two. Hardly surprising that it didn't go as planned the first time around. I report to the hospital at 5:30 am as I had done before. Things feel familiar this time and I'm not at all nervous. I get in my gown, and hop onto the hospital bed. When I speak with the nurse she tells me I'll be prepped for general anesthesia soon. I had been under the impression, after consulting with the anesthesia department in pre-op, that general wouldn't be necessary. I ask the nurse to double check the status of that. After three phone calls to Dr. Holt and the team, they finally agree that local anesthetic and "Twilight," as it's called, is sufficient.

When under "Twilight," you are technically awake mentally and able to be responsive, but heavily sedated and you don't remember anything when you come out of it. As we arrive in the operating room, one of the assistants inquires as to why I want my screws out, which starts a conversation about how my screws disagree with my work on the trapeze. Shortly thereafter I lose track of the conversation.

About 20 minutes later, I wake up mid-sentence cheerily inviting them all to AWOL's "Left of Center" show coming up the following weekend, though assuring them I am not going to be in it.

Before I left I asked if I could see the screws. They brought them for me to take home in a little plastic bag. I reached my hand in the bag, pulling out four remarkably shiny screws, the longest of which was five inches.

Left of Center

I'm okay, I'm okay, I'm okay. I'm sitting outside the AWOL warehouse in my car and I can't stop crying enough to go inside. I'm stage managing, and tonight is opening night of a three night run. I've been at tech and dress rehearsals all week keeping it together, trying not to let my mind spiral off. For the most part it's not too bad, I'm participating and involved which is better than "Art in the Dark" where I just went as a spectator. But if I let myself admit it, it's been tough. While the girls are in the dressing room laughing and doing make-up, I'm sweeping the stage. When they are on stage under the lights, I'm trying to be hidden while running the pulley line to fly them in the air. But tonight, in addition to those things, there will be an audience here and after the show they will run up and tell the girls how amazing and strong they all are. And I will feel invisible.

I don't mind sweeping the stage and we all help with rigging even when performing. What's making me sad is the separation I feel from not performing with the group. But now I'm upset because I'm having a pity party. Ugh! Why can't I just pull it together, walk in the door, and be happy with all the many things I have to be happy about? Am I creating this torment, is it possible to avoid? As everyone knows by now, shutting emotions away isn't very effective for me, but when does it end? I'm sick of the roller-coaster.

I text a friend who will be volunteering at the show tonight. She replies with some reassuring words, and mostly, compassion for what I must be feeling. That helped. When I go inside I get straight to work and avoid talking to anyone. If I talk to anyone I doubt I'll be able to hold back the flood of tears that I'm precariously on the verge of. I clean the stage, set up the rigging for the top of the show, and make sure the chairs are all in order. Each breath I take is deliberate and feels restricted.

Anatomy Riot

My hiding time is over when the house doors open and I have to be on and in action. The change of focus shifts my mood and I start to feel the buzz of the show. There are many familiar faces attending, including past students and our usual fans; it's nice to chat. I check in with the box office to see how many people we are waiting for. Then I check in with the dancers to let them know it's 10 minutes 'til curtain. Finally, I check that my headset is working and communicate to our sound booth that dancers are nearly ready and house is almost full. While I'm not in the show, the role of stage manager at least helps me feel like an integral part of the whole experience.

The show begins. Things are running smoothly. The dancers that aren't on stage help with the rigging, which includes running pulley lines up and down as needed to change out the aerial equipment for the upcoming pieces. When there's no rigging to be done we watch the show, pointing out our favorite parts of each piece and giggling at small mishaps that are funny to us, but go unnoticed by the audience.

Midway through the show there's a problem. We all see it. Some of our rigging lines have 3:1 pulleys while others have 1:1. The numbers simply refer to the distribution of weight load. While rigging, we always have to be careful of which lines have which pulleys, as lines with 3:1 pulleys have to be weighted or they will fly up and out of reach. That's exactly what happened on the front center point where just a light handloop is. I didn't see how it happened, but I immediately see that collectively and non-verbally the company is making a plan. I warn the man running the sound that he will need to loop the transition music and not to continue forward with the soundtrack until my go. In character, a few of the dancers make their way out on stage. Jess sits on Julie's shoulders while the others dance around distracting and trying to make it look like part of the choreography. The double stack gives Jess just enough height to reach the handloop as the other dancers assist in maneuvering her back to the ground and handing off the handloop to Jen and Sarah, who are now able to start their piece. I cue the music.

Backstage after the show, we are all laughing, recounting our thought process when each of us saw the imminent handloop disaster. Julie narrates how she made eye contact with Jess who had just looked up at the handloop and how they immediately moved onto stage knowing what had to be done. Everyone acknowledges that a potential crisis was averted and hopes the audience thought it was part of the piece. I felt fortunate to be there and backstage, reminded of that indescribable bond that I am a part of.

The show run concluded two nights later with no further mishaps. Each night, when mingling either before or after the show, I had many spouses of dancers, family members, and friends come up to me and say the show just wasn't the same without me. I appreciate their sentiment and will be in the next show, no matter how tiny my role is.

Right before the house doors opened on the last night, Jen called me back to the dressing room. When I opened the door I saw a big bouquet of flowers and the smiling faces of the whole company. While I knew they realized how hard this week was for me, this gesture meant a lot. More tears, they just don't seem to stop - happy or sad.

Moving on, moving out

<u>Journal Entry - May 6th, 2012</u>
I might be taking a huge leap of faith here shortly, but somehow it feels like the right decision. I decided to move out of the house I'm currently living in. The living situation stopped being what I wanted and needed. Among other things I guess I'm just looking for some peace and stability. The rent at the new place is twice what I pay now and I always seem to find myself struggling with money which makes me nervous. However, when my gut feeling is overpowering I often don't go with logic. Many times in life I have taken a risk and just made it work. I hope that's the case again.

Cleansing is the word. I went on a three day juice cleanse recently so I could erase the mental image of medication residue lingering in my system. Since entering the Positive Reinforcement Stage I have also been paying specific attention to things that are causing me unnecessary stress and trying to cleanse my world of those, too. I have been living in my current house for about two years. It's a lovely house with a front porch that gets morning sun and a delightfully pleasant backyard with lots of plants and a gazebo. The layout of the house is comfortable with plenty of open space, but there are three other housemates. Within the two years I've lived there, 10 different people have occupied the various rooms, and within the past year I became house manager so I handle signing of leases, paying and splitting of bills, coordinating the search for a new housemate, as well as turnover of the room. Quite frankly, I'm over it and ready for personal space. I want my as house clean as I left it. I want quiet time when I need it. Most of all, I don't want to manage anyone else's life but my own, which seems to be a big enough handful.

The apartment I just got my approval for today is utterly fabulous which is contributing to that gut feeling that it's the right decision to make. It's an upper unit, one bedroom that is part of a fourplex. The outside and the landscaping are well maintained and I even have a shared backyard for when I want to drink a beer in the grass this summer! The unit itself is quite charming, as well. You enter into the living room which leads into a dining room with a little nook I plan to turn into a study, then a spacious kitchen with a door to stairs that lead to the backyard. Continuing past the kitchen, you get to the bedroom and beyond that is my favorite part of all - a south facing sun room.

The whole apartment has beautiful hardwood floors that the landlord plans to refinish before I move in. The worn and dirty linoleum in the kitchen will be replaced with a slate colored tile floor, and he will paint the walls and offered to let me choose the paint colors. I have chosen a very neutral light brown with pinkish tints for the living/dining room, a lively butter yellow for the kitchen, and a calming blue for the bedroom. This will really feel like my very own space!!

The apartment is also in a different quadrant of town so I will have a welcomed change of scenery. The final noteworthy touch is an adorable little coffee shop just steps out the front door. I couldn't ask for more! While I'm a little nervous that it will keep me in my financially precarious place for longer, I feel like my sanity is an important consideration as well. I'm signing the lease tomorrow.

No more funding

<u>Journal Entry - May 12th, 2012</u>
I just got laid off from my job yesterday. I don't want to talk about it, think about, it or focus on it really, but I guess I'll write. I just want to be done asking for help or favors. I just want to be in a good place. I refuse to steal energy from the people who have been giving it to me for over a year now. I wish they would come to me with their problems so I can help them. I can't ask for help again. I can't help but wonder what life is trying to tell me with all this, but I don't think wondering will bring me an answer.

It's Friday and I have a meeting with my bosses at White Bird. One of them always refers to my job as "the plate spinner," referencing the circus act where the performer is tasked with keeping many plates spinning atop long poles. As usual, we begin the meeting by going over the list of plates we are trying to keep in motion. After systematically discussing the current status and next step of each item, we came to a pause. Each item has direct relevance to the budget and our overall bottom line. The end of the fiscal year is in June and there's been a concerning gap all year, making everyone nervous.

After a long pause, Walter says. "Emily, unfortunately we are no longer able to fund your position." For what seems like the millionth time in recent history all the blood drains from my body and I begin shaking. This just can't be happening. I don't even know how to react, resulting in a complete deficit in speaking ability. They both assure me that they appreciate my work and will be happy to help me find another job and/or give me positive recommendations. They will offer me severance pay and I will be welcome as their guest at any shows I want to see. Unfortunately, none of this makes me feel much better. I just went through the job hunt process almost exactly a year ago, and I know all too well the relentless ego wreckage that it incurs.

All I feel is defeat. There's no way I'm strong enough to do this again. I'm too numb to ask questions or do anything but accept what they're telling me and walk out the door. The reason I suddenly no longer have a job is irrelevant. What may come to pass in the future is irrelevant. All I can be sure of is the unfinished picture as it looks today: something like a deep, muddy puddle.

Journal Entry - May 19th, 2012
Tomorrow begins week two of no job. I'm trying so hard to stay positive, yet it's impossible to avoid some apprehension. I think letting go of the planning ahead is my best bet at sanity for now. I will find work, it may just take time. This time I want to be laid back. I want things to happen because they are meant to happen. I've just been struggling with the boundaries of that idea. For example: was I meant to find my amazing apartment to encourage that shift? Was I laid off specifically to open myself up to a next opportunity? I lean towards 'no' on both of these. Nothing is 'meant to be' it's just life happening. The people around me usually say I make good choices. The problem is, you rarely know what your actual choices are or what would have happened in a different scenario. Perhaps not knowing what could have been takes some of the weight off our choices because what we do choose is all we'll ever know.

Part Eight

Rhymes with bucket

Life goes on, that's all there is to it. I'm sick of being consumed by things out of my control so I'm now entering a "Rhymes with Bucket Stage." If ever-fluctuating circumstances is what life is giving me to work with, then I can't stop dead in my tracks every time a change in plans occurs. I just need to keep moving on as if it will all sort itself out. This logic is allowing me to continue forward with plans I made over a year ago - plans that to some may no longer seem "a good idea," but to me seem essential.

Back when I left Paris, my group of friends were all dispersing as well. Paneet moving back to London, Molly going to grad school at Oxford, Sam starting a clothing line and moving to Thailand, Nica getting her PhD in England, and Lucy moving to Egypt. There was something indescribably beautiful about our connection in Paris. We all arrived at nearly the same time from either the U.S. or England, and now we were all departing, moving on with our adventures. The night before Molly left - she was the first to have to say goodbye - we all had a sleepover. We gathered around Molly and my dining room table drinking wine and chatting. We also set up my computer and recorded the whole evening of conversation that went into the wee hours. We had an assignment prior to attending the sleepover to write down predictions about where each of us would be in three years. They included things like who would have kids, who would be famous and for what. It was equal parts serious and ridiculous.

It had been agreed upon that three years after our departure we would all meet up in Paris again for a reunion. On June 30th, 2011, at noon, we would meet at Le Progrès, the cafe in Montmarte where Sam, Paneet, and I first met. It was a somewhat silly and romantic idea, like in the movies, but each of us knew how special that moment would be.

Plans changed a bit over the course of the three years. Molly, who moved back to Paris, got engaged and we all agreed that the reunion would instead occur at her wedding. When my surgery was originally scheduled for May 6th, and her wedding was slated for May 29th, 2011, my heart broke knowing I wouldn't be able to make it. The girls all made space for me in the photos so they could photoshop me in later, but the fact was, I was the only one not there.

In August 2011, Paneet announced her engagement and hoped we would be able to make it to her wedding in England in July 2012. My plane ticket was booked in January and all hotel and train reservations were secured long before my job ceased. When faced with the decision of whether to cancel my trip or let life go on, I made the only choice I found acceptable.

From panic to grounding

I just stepped off the plane in Paris, on my way to England and it's completely surreal. It's 5:00 am and I've been traveling for 24 hours. Somehow, I'm supposed to make it through the day without sleeping so I can conquer jet lag. I hope the intense excitement of returning to Paris, as well as the anticipation of being with my dear friends again, will get me through the day.

While I didn't speak fluent French when I lived here, the familiarity of the sounds coming over the intercom is comforting. As I wait for my train to go meet Molly, several people timidly ask me for directions in broken French. Amazing! Maybe I look like I know what I'm doing and they think I'm Parisian. I was blonde when I lived here before and no one for a single moment mistook me for a local. Now that I'm brunette I guess I fit in a bit better, though the eye contact and smiling usually gives me away.

I just can't get over how dreamlike this feels. It's like visiting a past life. I feel flooded with clarity about the bigger picture. I feel connected to the strong, confident, risk taking person I was when I arrived here the first time. I physically feel the distance from Portland and my life and OHSU and my job search. I can suddenly imagine my friends' perspectives, watching me go through my last two years with this immense spacegap between us. Our worlds individually moving forward through detail, grit, joy, and swells on a parallel time table, yet with little ability to intersect. Skype, Facebook, and emails don't close the distance, they simply act as a window to another world. For a few moments I get to appreciate this distance from my world. Then the whirlwind begins.

Molly picks me up, we spend the day catching up and rushing around Paris. The next morning we train to London to meet Sam at the station, then on to pick up Nica who drives us north to the wedding location where we meet up with Paneet and Lucy, finally bringing the whole group together for the first time in four years. The excitement, the emotion, the exhaustion. We spend a whole week recollecting the distant past, catching up on the recent past, and embracing the present moment. Despite the distance that literally separated us for those years, my Paris girls made sure I felt their support and we picked up just where we left off.

I feel a sense of home in Europe. The foreign essence is familiar, and a part of my past, so not actually foreign anymore. I have friends and old jobs I could potentially go back to. It's strange, but I feel there could be a place for me here. Somehow it feels like there isn't a place for me in Portland right now. My intentions upon moving were clear and yet now seem confused. I'm floating. I'm free-falling. I have no attachments. My future could look like anything at this point. I'm trying to visualize what things will look like in Portland when the dust finally settles, but I have absolutely no trace of an image for that. I humor the thought of what things would look like if I just up and moved back to Europe, but wonder what would be my motivation, aside from trying to escape my presently tumultuous life.

I feel both grounded and panicked by these two thoughts. One of my favorite quotes is, "Leap and the net will appear," by John Burroughs. Being here reminds me that my net spans much wider than the small subsection of a view that exists right in front of me. Four years ago I dropped everything, moved to Paris, made friends, got jobs, had a boyfriend, built a life all in a mini time span of nine months, so why couldn't I do it all again if I felt like it? Maybe my options aren't as narrow as they often seem. But then panic sets in imagining that tricky line when "what-if" becomes a reality and the path unchosen is completely left behind. I can't handle that, I simultaneously want to live so many lives.

After an action packed yet emotionally rejuvenating trip, I come back to my senses. I am in no place to make another dramatic change. I adore my friends and they have helped me reconnect with a person I was four years ago. They have reminded me of how much I have accomplished in my time in Portland. They give me credit for the massive undertaking of going through with surgery and commend me on how well I've emerged, even if all the pieces aren't back in place. I can return home now with a goal to get back on my feet in order to scamper across the globe with them in miscellaneous adventures yet to be dreamed up.

From a slightly different angle, uncertainty can be exhilarating!

Soft steps

<u>Journal Entry - July 19th, 2012</u>
I'm going to try to encourage myself to be softer. When pushed out of a plane, perhaps being soft yourself is the only necessary answer because you don't know what the ground is going to look like when you arrive. It could be pavement or it could be clouds, but either way, if you are soft, the landing is at least guaranteed to have some give.

I'm in love with my apartment. The simple pleasure of returning home from rehearsal, pouring myself a glass of wine, and taking a long, hot bath with no disruption or need to interact with anyone is marvelous. A hundred moments a day I sigh with an appreciation for my own space. Also, for the first time in awhile, I feel genuinely okay with being alone. After glimpsing with Kalen how it felt to have a companion along for this journey, I've been saddened and concerned that that vacancy will never be filled. My friends promise me that the right person will enter my life at the right time, but I feel like that's just easy to say. Currently, I've made peace with my skepticism though. Whether it's the summer sun, an abundance of adventures with friends, distraction, or acceptance, it feels different. I don't dread being lonely.

And I'm back to dancing.

We started working on AWOL's annual "Art in the Dark" show back in May. The show is called "Drop of a Hat" and has a vintage circus theme. I was unanimously voted as the Magician, a character I know I'll have fun playing. While I will be in the show this time, I still need to be careful with what and how much I do so I have a small solo act and a few other appearances in dance pieces and as back up for other solo pieces. To help rebuild my strength I will be learning the group piece, which usually incorporates all 12 company members, but I will not be in the piece for the performance in case I run into restrictions with the choreography.

The group piece is spanish web or rope, which I've worked on before. The good news is that some of the other dancers haven't done much work on the rope so we will very much be learning from the beginning. On our first day of rehearsal I tried everything the rest of the company tried. First, we learned a little sequence where one hand was in a hand-loop at the top of the rope. We start in a hip lock, which I'm familiar with, and get a spin going. From the lock we then fan our legs out and drop to a fast pencil spin in the loop. Reaching out with the free hand we continue to spin around the rope making shapes with our legs. So far so good. My hip lock was a bit painful just because my body is no longer conditioned to the squeezing and the rope dug into my scar tissue, but nothing I felt would harm my body. My transitions were shaky as I still don't trust my physical ability 100 percent and my shapes were awkward, but the main point is that I could do all of it more or less.

In subsequent rehearsals we continued expanding upon that first section while adding another sequence with the right foot in the loop. Nothing challenged my restrictions of hip angle or straddle flexibility here either. Only at the end of the piece, when we had to get our foot out of the loop, was my inability to extend to a near split an issue. My version of the exit was significantly uglier than the rest of the group's, but I didn't need to worry about being performance-ready.

As the weeks progressed and some of the strain which is inevitably present when the movement is new, dissipated, my gap in ability seemed to narrow and I began to blend in with the group again.

Physical progressions

Believe it or not, my physical therapist is supportive of my ankle dangling. Since the screws came out, my body has leapt and bounded forward in the recovery process ... after the swollen, bloody bulge from the screw removal went away. Now, my scar tissue seems to be less persistent and more cooperative with the therapy. My hip angle or knee-to-chest range continues to improve with almost every visit. The one major hiccup that keeps returning is that the imbalance of right side versus left causes the two sides of my pelvis to twist in opposite directions. The right side hip flexor is stronger and the muscles surrounding more flexible than on the left side, rotating my right hip bone and pubic symphysis into an anterior tilt. Dangling by my right ankle, however, creates some traction to that joint which helps even things out.

Earlier on in my recovery, my pelvis snuck its way into this torsion regularly. I would then go in to physical therapy complaining that my Sacroiliac (SI) joint had sharp pain and my left leg felt like it was twisted and jammed up into the joint. To correct this, Maria needed an assistant to come push my pubic bone while she pulled my leg in the opposite direction. Depending on who was working, Maria would try to get a female to assist, but on occasion the only one available was a youngish man who turned bright red in the face when assigned the job. I personally have found it difficult to maintain any sense of modesty with the location of my injury, so instead I try to make light of it.

The other immensely helpful treatment for my wandering pelvic halves was wearing an SI Belt. The belt velcro's low around the hips, then is tightened with two other velcro flaps that hold the pelvis in a stable place. I have been wearing this in yoga, when I go walking, and when I do aerial. It's miraculous the effect it has in forcing the muscles that should be working to turn on, while keeping the balance on both sides.

Elusive policy

The only problem with physical therapy is that I have been paying for it out of my own pocket, and when I have to go twice a week, it's not cheap! I dread another battle with insurance, but I just can't believe that this is how the system works. I muster my energy.

<u>Notes from a conversation with insurance - August 25th, 2012</u>

Me: Hi I am hoping you can clarify a few things for me regarding my policy.

The Devil's secretary: Why certainly, how may I help you.

Me: I had a major hip surgery about nine months ago, it was quite intense and involved cutting the bone in my pelvis to restructure it and has involved a lengthy recovery. I am still in physical therapy and have reached my deductible, yet my insurance policy has still not contributed a dime towards my therapy.

The Devil's secretary: OK, let me take a look at your policy and explain your benefits. It looks like you have a $7,500 deductible and 20 physical therapy visits per calendar year. Once you've reached the $7,500 we pay 75% of the bill and you pay 25% up to $9,000 which is your yearly out of pocket maximum.

Me: Right however, my surgery was in late October of last year, though I wasn't able to begin physical therapy until the broken bone had healed in mid-December. Clearly with $100,000 surgery I reached my deductible last year, but was only able to get in five visits of PT before a new calendar year began and my deductible started over.

Now, since this January, I have paid out of pocket for all of my therapy, used all of my 20 per calendar year visits, shortly thereafter met my $7,500 again for the year and am still paying out of pocket for my PT.

The Devil's secretary: Well, I show here that the physical therapist provided an adjustment for you. For example, January 6th was your first visit this year and would have been $273, but they adjusted so you only paid $168.

Me: Yes, I am aware of that. So I paid out of pocket, my provider offered me a discount for paying out of pocket, and insurance took absolutely none of the responsibility for assuring I received proper health care for my recovery.

The Devil's secretary: Well ... yes ... let me pull up some more information.

Me: Look perhaps it's a fundamental flaw in the system itself, but I just don't understand how you can authorize a major surgery but then refuse to assist me through my full recovery. What options do I have? Do I have any? Is restoring my body to health no concern if you can get out of paying for it?

The Devil's secretary: If I were you, though I am not allowed to advise you, but if I were you, I would file an appeal.

Me: OK, tell me more about that.

The Devil's secretary: Do you have access to internet?

Me: Yes, I have my account opened on my screen as we speak.

The Devil's secretary: If you look under forms you will find one entitled Member Appeal Form. You can fill that out and you will also need to fill out the Authorization for Appeals. You'll then need to get documentation from your doctor showing medical necessity and the severity of your surgery to indicate that you need additional coverage. You should probably get a letter from your physical therapist as well.

Me: Let's back up. I am unable to find the second form you mentioned.

The Devil's secretary: What page are you looking at?

Me: I am in my account looking under forms.

The Devil's secretary: Go ahead and open a new tab at the top of your page and I'll direct you to another site, sometimes the forms are unavailable in your version of the site.

Hmmm, hardly surprising that a necessary form that would allow me to make an appeal is not readily available to me. The world of insurance is outrageous. When I am finally directed to the forms, she walks me through each one and tells me which sections I will need to fill out. I need to write a brief description of my appeal and submit my supporting documentation from the surgeon and therapist, indicating that physical therapy is still necessary in my recovery. She also says be very specific about what I ask for, but is unable to be more clear in advising me on what that means. When I give an example, she says she is not allowed to give me any further guidance. She just keeps repeating, *"Be specific on what you're asking for."*

***

Despite submitting an appeal which included both a letter from my doctor and a letter from my therapist along with a clear description of what I was asking for (simply for insurance to pay a portion of my recovery costs), the appeal was denied. This time around, I don't have it in me nor possess additional tools to fight back.

Showtime

August 26th, 2012

    We usually set up our stages about three weeks before the show so we can rehearse in the park. Our aerial apparatus is on cables strung between the trees and since the cables have some stretch that the beams in the warehouse don't have, it's always a surprise to see what aerial pieces will need to be reworked to accommodate. The first two weeks we rehearse with a small portable stereo and in the near dark (aside from a few work lights). The week before the show we add full theatre lights and an official sound system. The anticipation always builds the week before the show when we get to light up the forest and the magic of "Art in the Dark" becomes tangible again.

    Finally it's Friday, opening night, and the company arrives at the park at noon to start set up. Doors don't open until 7:30 pm, but we need to rope off the performance area, place signs along the road, set up the entrance and front of house, set up concessions, sweep the stages, and pre-set all rigging for the top of the show. After all the logistics we will still need time to eat and get hair, make-up and costumes on so there's no time to waste!

    It's a beautiful sunny day and the forecast for the weekend has been kind enough to eliminate any additional stress of potential rain. After all the prep work is complete, we go out for a group dinner and fill ourselves with salads, sandwiches, quesadillas - each dancer has her own preference to what will sustain her for the evening without weighing her down.

    Back at the park, we sit outside our dressing room (a horse trailer) at picnic tables and do our hair and make up. For this show we are using an airbrush to make white accents on our faces. Since I'm the magician, I have a card trick on my face - well, it's really just an airbrushed playing card but someone decided it would be funnier to say, *there's a card trick on your face!* Same as every night this week, I have to make a rectangle out of masking tape that goes around one eye so the paint has clean edges. Then I use black liquid liner to outline the edge and draw a club on two corners. The girls always laugh at me when I'm sitting there with my face taped up waiting for my turn to be airbrushed, but the tape doesn't allow my cheeks to smile so I am forced to respond with a deadpan look. Paulina is the poodle and Sarah is the lion, so their white airbrush accents are right around their mouths. We like to tease them when the white mouth is the only part of their makeup that's finished, and accuse them of getting into a bag of powdered donuts.

There is a constant stream of conversation from show talk, to banter, to shouts of, "Brandy I need your lip liner....where's the eyelash glue?....Kelsey, did you try to steal my sparkles again!" As Eek is helping me determine placement for my tiny top hat, I see Paulina and Sarah at the corner of one of the picnic tables with intentionally sheepish grins, nibbling on powdered donuts, waiting for someone to notice them. I shriek and point, and everyone looks. Paulina and Sarah are laughing the hardest at their own joke.

The closer it is to showtime, the louder and rowdier we get. Crammed in the trailer trying to get our costumes on, any passersby must wonder what is going on in there. Our stage manager gives us the 10 minute warning and we all do last minute stretches and preparations for the show.

I know a number of people in the audience tonight. It felt so good to tell people about "Art in the Dark" this summer because when they asked if I'd be performing, I could definitively say, "YES! Look for the Magician!" The other exciting thing is that when the group rope piece was finalized, I was given a part so it will truly be a full company piece.

The energy produced by this show is unreal. When you drive down the dark road away from the city to come upon the forest lit with color, grab a bag of popcorn, and nestle in under the stars, you know you're about to witness something special. And when the show begins both dancers and audience members alike share in the enchanting adventure that is "Art in the Dark." For the duration of the show, my focus is nowhere but in the present moment and I am filled with an infinite feeling of happiness.

After the show some of my former students who were in the audience tell me how proud they are of me and that they're so happy to see me performing again. They promise they never would have known I had a broken pelvis less than year ago. Another group of friends comes to say hello, and two of them have hardly seen me since my first six weeks post surgery. They chuckle with disbelief at how they once brought me ice cream and had to carry it to the table for me as I hobbled along behind with my walker and now I'm 20 feet in the air, hanging by my ankles, and managing to look, at least to their eyes, like I never missed a beat.

I'm intoxicated with the feeling of performing my first show back since surgery. It will definitely not be my last!

Still not whole

September 2012

    Summer is dwindling to an end, and now it seems all I have to focus on is getting a job, which is the biggest remaining unfinished piece. I'm back teaching about two thirds of a full schedule now, so I am able to barely sustain myself financially while I continue sorting. I know it's a bad idea to rely on my physicality for the majority of my income. Even if it were accessible, I feel very absolute with the choice to continue to find a balance and look for office work. I have applied for many jobs and had interviews that have gone very well, leaving me both surprised and frustrated when at the end of the day, I'm still searching. Sometimes I wonder if the organizations I'm applying for can hear the desperation in my cover letter. I wonder if they are scoffing at my eclectic resume when they have 200 other applicants who have been building their career directly towards the exact job description for over a decade. Since "Development Specialist" is the last title I held, I've been applying for similar positions with various Portland arts organizations. It's no question that I fully support the arts and can generate a compelling argument for the value of arts as a general field.

    Somehow though, it all feels distant from what I know and where my heart is. As I've already established, I feel out of place in an office, so that doesn't really help my visualization of how it will all work out. Ultimately, I wonder why I have this deep sense that I don't even want the jobs I'm applying for. Struggling with my gut feelings is usually a red flag, but I can't seem to locate an alternative option.

<u>Email exchange with my friend Sara - October 12th, 2012</u>

Me: And once again my trust and hope were shattered into tiny, tiny pieces so small it's hard to imagine them ever fitting back together.

The job market is brutal. Twice now, I have been recruited for and offered a job that later suddenly drops off the table, no reason, no warning. It just makes me so disillusioned and confused. I don't feel like I can trust that anything will work out because I continually gather up my positive attitude only for things to ultimately fall through time after time.

Sara: Well, shit. I bet disillusioned is an understatement. I feel as though it's a shitty odds game that requires bashing one's head against the effing wall because, one of these times, that head will crash through into ... I don't know, a beautiful meadow full of fun and excitement and income. But it's counterintuitive to everything to keep the bashing, let alone be so optimistic while you do it. I'm sorry you're having to deal with this yet again!

Me: Thank you for speaking my language! Bashing and crashing and effing walls and the counterintuitive nature of it all! I'm so sick of keep your chin up and descriptions of that light happy place that will exist some other time. Because it doesn't exist now and now is what I'm working with!!!

Money

<u>Journal Entry - September 26th, 2012</u>
I had a realization yesterday that doesn't seem that profound in fact. Quite simply, I have never valued money, which is probably the exact reason I struggle with financial stability. If I did value or prioritize money, I would have made many choices differently thus far and I imagine it wouldn't be such a constant issue today. In your 20's it's perfectly acceptable to just get by, but now that I'm in my 30's, I have been hoping to do more than that. I want to be past a place of panicking when I need new tires, I want to be able to take a friend to dinner just as a treat, I want to donate to organizations having realized the importance of individual support within nonprofits. I also want to continue practicing a "Plentitude"[2] lifestyle of: work less do more for yourself. I already do this by mostly eating at home, trading for services when possible (Pilates for acupuncture, aerial lessons for tax preparation), and living a fairly minimalist lifestyle. The other things I value most are: socializing, traveling, fitness and health. I don't think this is out of reach but I do need to find the right combination to achieve it.

---

[2] "Plentitude" is a book written by Juliet B. Schor. A highly recommended read!

Two things

Thing one: I've started therapy in hopes that someone else can help me sort through the mess that's going on inside my head. I need a consistent and focused outside perspective giving me insight as to where I'm missing the boat. My first day of therapy I didn't even know where to start the story. It's taken a good three or four sessions for my therapist to even be able to understand what I'm seeking, but I have been benefitting from it since day one. I don't care if you're the most sane person on earth, the opportunity to have someone's undivided attention picking up on the language you choose and the patterns you dwell on is astonishingly revealing. My therapist has helped me understand the conflict of interest in my desire for a paycheck as my sole focus, in contrast to my inclination to follow my passion regardless of financial gain. She has pointed out that the places where my goals and my actions stem from are such dramatically different places, they will never meet. She then guides me toward reworking my perspective on each so they eventually have the potential to align. She forced me to stop blaming myself for everything that's gone wrong, and gently reminded me how ludicrous an idea it is in the first place. I hope that in time, logic and my gut instincts will meet on the same page, divulging the path to a not-so-messy future.

Thing two: I've been writing. This isn't new, in fact I began writing in April 2012. I've kept it so secret I almost don't admit to myself I'm doing it. It all started when a former Adidas yoga student and I were having a conversation after a class I taught post surgery. She was inquiring about things that most people don't think to ask, specifically, the emotional side effects of making a decision like I did and going through with it. She emphasized that there is a weighty portion of the story that is rarely told, but is too important to go unacknowledged. Clearly, I agreed. The surgery portion of the story seemed to be only the tip of the iceberg, yet topics about emotional status, financial well-being, loss of identity, etc., are rarely part of the public story. At the end of the conversation, she encouraged me to write a book. I chuckled at the thought of such an undertaking and was sure that no one would actually read it. But the idea became a voice in the back of my head that kept nagging me to see what would happen if I just picked up a pen. So one day I planted myself in a cafe with a bottomless mug of black coffee to see what would happen. It was a story with a life of its own and seemed to just pour out of me.

Then a miraculous thing happened. Once on the page, the story no longer had to live inside my body. I had been keeping the details safe inside so I would never forget. I wanted desperately to move on, but I was unwilling to let this defining personal moment be lost in the past.

I have no idea how the book will end or what will come of it then. But I do know that the process of writing it has been fueling my creativity and reminding me of the journey I have made as well as who I was along the way.

What I know

<u>Journal Entry - October 14th, 2012</u>
I just had the most amazing conversation with Paneet. First, she is one of the most nurturing, genuine, caring individuals I've ever met. Her calmness and composure always cuts through any irrationalities, panic, frustration, or anger I might be expressing and manages to steer my focus back to what's underneath. She told me I'm one of the strongest people she knows, but reminded me again and again that I put too much pressure on myself and that the self critic always gets in the way of me seeing the whole picture and giving credit to myself where it's due.

Our discussion reminded me of a boundary where effort intensifies to a place of force and no longer becomes helpful or productive. I know this about myself. I have always felt that if I wanted something I could get it, not just that it would and should come to me, but if I was proactive, resourceful, genuine, and passionate I could make it happen. I have been proven correct on this many times which has built up my confidence. But there have been other times where, despite my efforts and intentions, things aren't working out and this is where I dangerously cross into the territory of force. While this isn't a new discovery for me, I think this conversation and context woke me up to the thought that the part I do have control over is whether to cross that boundary, which inevitably leads me to a state of distress. The word Paneet kept coming up with, and what she assigned me to think about, is 'release.' I hope that this one simple word can be that answer or direction I crave when I just want something to hold on to. A guide to how I should behave, react, prioritize. It actually goes quite well with what I need right now which is just ease. I don't want to charge into a new professional endeavor where I'm intimidated and unsure of myself. I don't want to turn over the lifestyle of flexibility I've known my whole life. I want to follow my gut without over-analyzing. To regain trust in my capacity to make decisions. To regain confidence with who I am and what I have to offer. To find a place where I don't blame my flaws for the things that are challenging me right now. Release expectation, release pressure, release the voice of the inner critic. Allow the personal balance to re-emerge and follow it forward.

New list

October 31st, 2012

It's one year past surgery and almost two since this whole process began. I've decided to revise my list. I'm 31 and so far I've:

-pursued the artistry of independence.

-reinvented myself time and again to keep up with the changing images in my dreams.

-allowed myself to love, and valued the people around me.

-faced a major life change and emerged with a sense of the beauty that can lie amongst grit.

But mostly, I've been me all along.

EPILOGUE

An idea

December 19th, 2012

    I press "send" on another job application, and similar to previous positions I've applied for, I can't figure out why it just doesn't feel right. It's an arts related job. The organization has some exciting international components that I think are pretty cool. A big part of their mission is also to build community which I appreciate a lot. I admit I was excited about it for a fleeting moment, but the gut feeling that this isn't the job for me is just too overpowering.

    I've been working with my therapist to figure out what is missing from these jobs, but I haven't quite put my finger on it. I moved to Portland in hopes that it was a place where leaders, who have both the desire and the capacity, are able to shape the future of the community. Upon arriving, I came across AWOL with whom I was able to build an education program that continues to thrive today. When circumstances changed, I found White Bird, where my knowledge of, and exposure to, the dance community grew considerably. Working with each company was exhilarating in its own way. With AWOL I felt like I was truly creating something of value that would have a lasting impact both on the company and the community. With White Bird, I was able to be surrounded by dance - the best in the world - and it was my job to advocate the importance of their mission to the community.

    As I sit at the cafe below my apartment, pondering my feeling of defeat at ever securing new work that suits me, an idea pops into my head. While living in LA, I was a member of an organization called the Dance Resource Center of Greater Los Angeles. They are a service organization dedicated to unifying and promoting all dance activity in Southern California.

They provide a single point of access to information, resources, and services relevant to dancers and the dance community.

I quickly rack my brain for anything like this that exists in Portland and come up with nothing. I begin visualizing what it would look like for me to originate something similar here. I went through the process of developing my own business, "Movement Inspired," and through my experience with AWOL and White Bird my list of skills seems to align directly with those I would need to take on such an endeavor.

Suddenly, I begin feeling either very caffeinated or very excited! Instead of a red flag, my gut feeling seems to be saying *ding ding ding!* But that's terrifying and ludicrous! I am supposed to be on a break from taking big risks. I'm supposed to be playing it safe, allowing for some calm in my life. I leave the cafe and take a walk. My thoughts, cells, and intuition seem to be jumping about despite me.

***

Over the course of the next few months I introduce my big idea to a few people who I consider professional mentors. I give them ample opportunity to tell me that I'm nuts, that it's too big of an endeavor for me to take on, and with too many risks. To my surprise, support and encouragement are the only responses I receive. Before long I have recruited an advisory board, written an executive summary, done extensive research on the viability of creating such an organization, and learned about various business models that would allow the organization to be sustainable. With everything in order, my next step is to secure funding and turn this into my next official career progression.[3]

---

[3] Please go to www.dancewirepdx.org to see how it turns out!

A new main character

The same day I had my big idea I also went on a date with someone named Andy. I met him for a drink later in the evening after I finished rehearsal. We drank hot toddies and had pleasant conversation. The evening was fairly short and as it ended we agreed to see each other again after the Christmas holidays.

On our second date we went cross country skiing. He picked me up in the morning, paid for my ski rental on the way up to the trail, and drove us up to a snowy lake on Mt. Hood. We skied in to the lake where the sun was sparkling off the bright snow. He had packed a lunch for us and we ate our sandwiches while being dive bombed by hungry birds in the trees. On the way home there was a traffic jam coming down from the mountain and we spent nearly four hours in the car, yet when we got back to town, he suggested we have dinner together.

Over the course of the day we seemed to cover quite a number of subjects. I found myself telling him about my business idea and my writing. While the fact that I was writing a book I had finally made public a few months prior, I had told almost no one about my business. Yet, I felt like I had nothing to lose as I hardly knew him, and it was supposed to be part of this new identity I was creating. I figured I should try it out. I expected him to do what most people do and overlook those things and ask, "Is that how you make a living?" Instead, he simply wanted to learn more.

He is a 5th and 6th grade teacher, and one of the core subjects he teaches is Language Arts, so he was curious about my creative process with writing, and asked many detailed questions. He is also a songwriter and plays the guitar. Our conversation would jump from my writing to his writing, to his music to my dancing. Often when you are first getting to know someone the dynamic is more like, inform and receive information. With Andy it felt like a shared dialogue.

We continued to see each other more often. He seemed sweet, mature, a good communicator, and not predetermined either way of how he wanted things to go. It was easy and comfortable, but I was very aware that I was being vulnerable again, potentially playing with fire; I still didn't feel strong enough to deal with another disappointment. Even still, walking away in fear did not seem worth it, so I did my best to just be cautious. He was cautious too, still in the process of moving on from a past relationship.

On Saturday mornings he would drop me off at therapy and I would joke, "Always a good sign when you have to drop your girlfriend off at therapy!" It was the lack of discomfort that made it funny. It had been impossible to avoid revealing the dark moments of my recent past since they still lingered with me.

I remember one day I had asked him about his last relationship and he wanted to hear the story about Kalen. I told him a brief version of the story which ended with my remaining confusion of how anyone could be so careless with someone knowing what a fragile place they were in. Andy didn't say anything, he just wrapped his arms tightly around me and held me close to him. He didn't let go for awhile, and I felt our respective caution beginning to melt away.

I'm sure he had his own little turning points, but it was clear that we were gradually, yet simultaneously opening up to the emotions we were feeling about each other. I know this because we talked about it. I know this because the doubt I have felt in the past, that at the time I chose to overlook, was not present this time. Not two months into our careful progression towards a relationship we were on a weekend trip together. We were going cross country skiing again and I was giggling at the map because a trail that was probably supposed to be labeled, "Snow Shoe," appeared as, "Snows Hoe." Andy just shook his head and said, "That's one of the things I love about you, you are able to entertain yourself better than anyone I know." I looked over and his eyes told me that he meant the words he chose. It had been a long time since I had even been able to love anything about myself and I realized that I truly felt happy. I even felt carefree, able to laugh foolishly at a typo on the map, not weighed down by deeply rooted concerns about who I was, what I was doing, and how things would fit together.

I think you're supposed to keep the ones that draw out the best in you and appreciate you for who you are.

Journal Entry - May 8th
I continue to be swept away.

Impermanence

It would be impossible for me to neatly wrap this story in a package for you. My hip still has limitations, though the pain is mostly gone and my ultimate goal of getting back to a high level of physicality was fulfilled. Financial security is largely a myth, and I haven't changed my relationship with money, maybe just my perspective. My business is still a risk, yet to be lived out, but my heart is behind it and my gut is on board. And love will always be love both fragile and unique.

Though I originally wrote this in a state of grief, I will leave us all with this thought:

Recognize the impermanence of both joy and sadness, be consumed by neither, and find peace in the balance that comes with fluctuation.

ACKNOWLEDGEMENTS

My first thanks absolutely must go to my parents for continuing to be supportive of me, regardless of how seemingly impractical some of my endeavors may be. I never would have had the courage to go through with some of my more risky ideas without feeling like on some level you trusted in me. And to my sister for being a more practical voice that I can bounce things off of, but also someone who always has my best interest in mind. To Louisa for letting me call you and just cry, allowing me to experience my grief and then helping to build my mental and emotional strength back. To Becky for letting Mom and I take over your house for a month. It was such a treasure to be able to spend that time with family. To Lulu for being such a valuable resource, and Jim for his manual labor. To all the other extended family who kept me in their thoughts and prayers.

To my Portland friends, students and colleagues, thank you for being there and continuing to buoy me through my tough moments, bringing me laughs, joy and inspiration. To my Paris friends, thank you for never letting me forget you were there, and keeping me connected to the person I felt like was "me" before all this happened. To my Los Angeles and Missoula friends, you also helped me feel grounded and reminded me of all the steps I've taken to get where I am.

Patty Goffe, I have no idea if this is anything like what you envisioned when you suggested I write a book, but it's what came out and I am eternally thankful that you made the suggestion. The act of writing brought so much healing and has been one of the most influential aspects in helping me move forward.

To Lisa Walser and Parker Huey, my official editors. It was a complete honor to have your red pen grace my pages.

To Mom, Sara Walker and Andy Bardeschewski, my unofficial editors, thank you for reading, rereading and discussing my work with me with care and honesty, and for humoring my endless requests to predict if anyone would ever read it. To Hannah Moore for helping me design the cover and remaining in good spirits as we revised until both happy with the product. And to Pil-oga-robic for the use of your space.

I'd also like to thank my physician and surgeon, both of whom are recognized in this book under alias names. I am genuinely touched by the level of compassion and individualized care I received. A true blessing, especially within the context of the circumstances.

And to anyone I've missed, there are so many important people in my life, I don't have the pages.

ADDITIONAL RESOURCES

My website: www.movementinspired.com

DanceWire: www.dancewirepdx.org

International Hip Dysplasia Institute: www.hipdysplasia.org

The following images were graciously provided by the International Hip Dysplasia Institute. In my research I discovered IHDI which became an invaluable resource in helping me learn about and understand my diagnosis and recommended procedure. Please refer to www.hipdysplasia.org for more information.

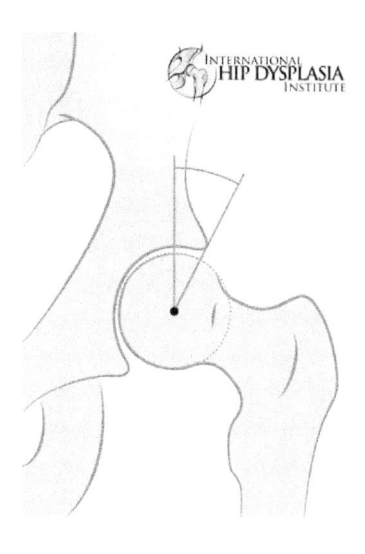

This image illustrates the center-edge angle, relating to the center of the femoral head and the outer edge of the acetabulum. A normal hip has an angle of 25 degrees or more. My left hip had a center-edge angle of 17 degrees, and my right 23 degrees.

Periacetabular Osteotomy

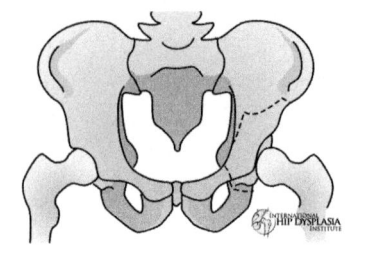

First the bone is cut

Then the acetabulum (hip socket) is rotated.

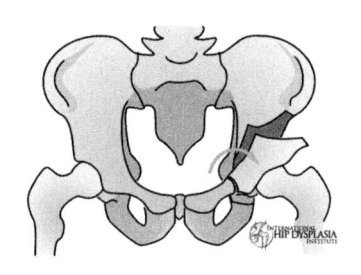

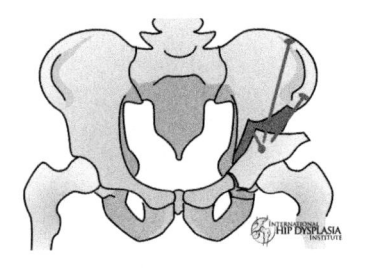

The new positioning is held together with screws.

The bone heals with a new center edge angle that preserves the integrity of the joint.

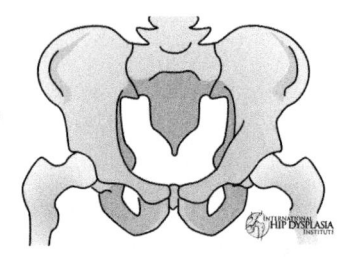

Printed in Great Britain
by Amazon

81411395R10122